Europe:
More than a Continent

Europe:
More than a Continent

MICHAEL BUTLER

HEINEMANN : LONDON

William Heinemann Ltd
10 Upper Grosvenor Street, London W1X 9PA
LONDON MELBOURNE
JOHANNESBURG AUCKLAND

First published 1986
© Sir Michael Butler 1986
ISBN 0 434 09925 2

Set in 10/13pt Plantin light by Deltatype, Ellesmere Port
Printed in Great Britain by Billing & Sons Ltd., Hylton Road, Worcester

Contents

Introduction

DURING MY SIX years as British Permanent Representative to the European Community in Brussels, I spent much time trying to explain the Community to audiences in Britain and to visitors from Britain. It was an uphill struggle. The structure of the Community is not easy to understand and the subjects it deals with so many and complex that it cannot be encapsulated.

Whether we like it or not, the Community is now part of our national life. Together with Westminster and Whitehall, with County and District Councils, it forms part of the government of the United Kingdom. Government rests on the consent of the governed. No one can easily consent to something of which they are ignorant. And yet ignorance of the Community prevails. There is a great need for the politicians, diplomats, journalists, lawyers, and specialists of every kind who see the Community at work to tell others what it is and how it works. Not enough is being done. I have therefore decided to continue the uphill struggle a little longer and to make a more comprehensive effort to explain it before I forget.

Readers and critics have a right to know at the outset where the author stands. I stand convinced of the need for European unity. This conviction has been growing rather than decreasing for the last quarter of a century, despite the fact that the working methods of the Community are often painful to the participants and have a tendency to foster cynicism in those who suffer them for too long. Now that I have left Brussels, I rejoice in my liberation from the eternal round of meetings and the grind of understanding the nitty-gritty of endless complicated subjects. But I remain unrepentant in advocating the need for the work to be done, and done well. In my view, the unity of the Community in the world is essential to the prosperity and wellbeing of European people, including British people. It is one of the great issues of this last quarter of the twentieth century.

Those, therefore, who do not want to know anything good about the European Community and who hate the very idea of a Common Market should

1

not attempt to read this book. It may give them some ammunition for attacking the Community, because I do not conceal its faults and weaknesses; but it will also give them apoplexy. They should stop now. But those who believe that all ought to be sweetness and light in Brussels and that a touch less nationalism on the part of Mrs Thatcher or President Mitterrand would allow the Community to develop rapidly towards a federation without internal quarrels will also find the reality, as I see it, unattractive.

No living and working part of government is ever sweetness and light. To be convinced of the need for European unity cannot in the real world of politics and economics require politicians, industrialists, farmers, scientists or consumers to give up fighting for their national or group interests. Even in a united country, except in wartime, they do not do that. The life of the Community is not destined to be easy or uncontroversial, any more than political life in Washington or Canberra, Paris or Rome.

This book is not about me. I shall try my best not to appear too often in the story. But the theme of European unity has been with me throughout the thirty-five years of my Foreign Office career and so I propose in this introduction to recount briefly how, when and why I became a convinced 'European'. The past may help to illuminate the present.

I joined the Western European Department of the Foreign Office in June 1950. Although the Treaty setting up the European Coal and Steel Community (the first post-war institution devoted to the cause of European unity and with Euratom and the EEC the basis of the present European Community) was being negotiated between France, Germany, Italy and Benelux, as its founder members, no one in the Foreign Office then seemed to think it odd that Britain was not to be a member. It is true that Sir Winston Churchill, in his famous Zürich speech, espoused the cause of European unity in 1946, but he was ambivalent on the subject of whether he saw Britain as part of a united Europe. I expect that, if they had been asked, most members of the Foreign Office would in 1950 have agreed with the basic thesis of Jean Monnet and the Founding Fathers of the Community that France and Germany must never fight each other again and that the most certain way of making this impossible was to unite their economies and to build the United States of Europe. But equally, in 1950, it was still fashionable to think of Britain as a Great Power, one of the Big Three with the United States and the Soviet Union. France, defeated in the war and still struggling back towards prosperity under the Fourth Republic, with governments changing every few months, was certainly not regarded as Britain's equal. Germany was still very much under four-power tutelage. Even among the young diplomats of the post-war generation, there were few who felt that Britain was missing the bus by staying out of the ECSC.

Few people now remember that a European Defence Community of the Six was almost created in 1954, a step which would have – at least in appearance – been a still greater step towards a united Europe than the EEC itself, created in 1958 by the Treaty of Rome which was signed on 25 March 1957. The EDC Treaty, providing for real integration of the defence forces of France, Germany and Italy and the Benelux, was agreed by the governments and only failed in the French National Assembly. Britain never seriously considered joining.

I remember the stirring of doubt in my mind about the wisdom of our posture. People seemed to assume that it was out of the question for Britain to give up 'sovereignty' on the scale required. Yet had we not already given up a huge slice of that allegedly precious commodity in the defence field when we signed the Nato Treaty? The decision of the French National Assembly, based in large part on a gut feeling on the sovereignty point, made it easy, however, to set the question aside for the time being.

Meanwhile, I was living in New York, posted in September 1952 to be private secretary to Sir Gladwyn Jebb (later Lord Gladwyn) who was then Permanent Representative at the UN. It was the period of the Cold War – and the Korean War. The Russians were behaving in such an intolerable way that the solidarity of Western Europe and the United States seemed a natural and essential element in world affairs. I was by upbringing pro-American and I liked living in New York. But I had not been there six months before I became conscious for the first time that I was a European. It was partly nostalgia for European architecture, for old churches and city centres, and for the centuries-old agricultural landscape of Britain or France; partly distaste for gas stations, ribbon development and endless advertising. But although I had not yet lived in any other European country, I had also already a feeling that European culture in its widest sense was very different from American. This came as a surprise to me at the time. I had been brought up to think that Britain, America and the white Commonwealth were composed of like-minded people. But I realised then and have always felt since that I was more at home in Paris, Brussels or even Rome than in Washington, New York, or Boston, let alone Houston or Los Angeles.

The UN, where a world game of diplomacy was played every day, also revealed an important fact to me. Not only was the world divided into two camps, East and West, grouped around the two super-powers – with the Third World then relatively unimportant – but the American super-power was prone to pay extremely little attention to the views of its European allies. We and the

3

French found ourselves often working together, not all that effectively, to influence American policy. Despite all the talk of a 'special relationship' between Britain and America, the UK on its own did not cut much ice.

I left New York in August 1956 and arrived in my next post, Baghdad, two weeks before the Anglo-French military action over the Suez Canal. I was among those instinctively opposed to Suez, partly because I believed that it was necessary to strengthen rather than weaken the international rule of law, but still more because it seemed to me that even if we were successful the expedition would be contrary to our interests. We had been on the Canal until two years before and had not found it convenient to stay there against Egyptian opposition. We were helping Nasser rather than hindering him in his quest for xenophobic Arab unity. But all that is another story. What Suez brought home in the most striking way was the relative impotence of middle-sized European countries in the post-war world. It completed the process of convincing me that the British Government ought to be working for European unity with Britain inside. And I believe that Suez did in fact play an important part in convincing Mr Harold Macmillan, the Conservative Party and the British people of the need to join the European Community. But unfortunately, work on the drafting of the Treaty of Rome was already well advanced. (If Suez had happened a year or two earlier, perhaps its lessons could have been learned in time!) Britain again stayed outside, and we missed a still more important bus.

Early in 1961 Mr Harold Macmillan, who had already decided to take Britain into the EEC, appointed Sir Pierson Dixon to be Ambassador to Paris, with the thought in mind that he would play a major role in the forthcoming negotiations. (He was duly appointed leader of the official team in the 1961-63 negotiations in Brussels under Mr Edward Heath when they opened – a role which in the light of hindsight could not be sensibly combined with the Embassy in Paris because of the need for the leader of the team to be in London helping to get the negotiating instructions right.) He had been my Ambassador in New York from 1954 to 1956 and to my great delight he asked the Foreign Office to send me with him to Paris to deal with European affairs. And so I began my long '*servitudes et grandeurs européennes*'. General de Gaulle's opposition to European integration and his veto of our membership in January 1963 left me even more determined that it was in the interests of Europe as well as Britain that the Community should prosper with Britain as a member.

It was at about this time that the economic arguments in favour of a large European market began to impinge on my consciousness. I had read PPE at Oxford in 1948-50, specialising in Economics under Tony Crosland at Trinity, and had always been interested in national and international economic questions. I had been very often with Bob Dixon to visit Jean Monnet and he had always stressed the economic case for creating a single market in Europe to match the great market in the United States if the European economies were to prosper in the long run. Economics joined politics in my mind as another essential reason for creating a united Europe.

I returned to London in 1965, no longer working directly on European affairs. But though I continued my keen interest in the subject, I did not too much regret my lack of a direct role in the Wilson Government's second attempt to join the Community in 1966-67. My experience in Paris had convinced me that we would now have to wait until de Gaulle left power.

In 1968, I was posted to the British Mission to the international organisations in Geneva, including EFTA and GATT, which was useful training for my later career. But when, in 1969, de Gaulle lost his referendum and went back to Colombey-les-Deux-Eglises and the way seemed open for us to make a successful application to join the Community, I felt that Geneva was very much on the fringes of where the important action was going to lie. I wrote to the Foreign Office to ask them to bear in mind my interest and my desire to play a role in any new negotiations. But they replied that they wanted me to take the Fellowship offered to the Foreign Office each year at the Center for International Affairs at Harvard in September 1970. I wrote back to say that, in my view, the time had come for action, not thought. But they were not to be moved. They said that I could concentrate on European affairs at Harvard. I did as I was told, went to Harvard and wrote a paper on the case for a European Defence Community as one of the pillars of the Atlantic Alliance and an essential element in the long-term industrial development of Europe in the face of the American Challenge. Defence joined politics and economics in the case for European Unity.

I made it clear to the Foreign Office that I wanted to get back into the European stream as soon as I left Harvard. They responded, not as I had hoped by posting me to the entry negotiations team, but by removing me from Harvard early and sending me to be the Counsellor in charge of European and Alliance matters in the Embassy in Washington.

But in March 1972 chance changed my fortunes and profoundly influenced the last fifteen years of my career. John Mason, later to be High Commissioner in Australia, who had been appointed only a few months before to be Head of the European Integration Department which dealt with the Community, saw an opportunity for promotion on secondment to the Export Credits Guarantee Department and decided to take it. A new Head of the Department was needed. I was ski-ing with my wife in Utah in late March 1972 when the

Embassy rang to say the Foreign Office wanted me to take the job. I accepted immediately and returned to London in June 1972. My first tasks were to help prepare for our entry on 1st January 1973 and to finish the negotiations between the European Community and the EFTA countries which led to the gradual creation of a free trade area covering nearly the whole of Western Europe.

Since then the Community has taken up most of my life. In January 1974, I was promoted to be the Under-Secretary in charge of it, just in time gloomily to prepare the pre-election contingency papers for the so-called renegotiation of the terms of entry which formed part of the Labour Party's Manifesto for the February Election.

I remember that, on the first day of the new Labour Government in 1974, Mr Callaghan called me to his office and said that he wanted to have a brief word with me straight away. No Private Secretary was present, which was unusual. He had read my contingency minute which analysed the points in the Manifesto which would be relatively negotiable in Brussels and those which might not and suggested that there were certain things which, if done in the first week or two of the new Government, would improve the chances of success and others seriously damage it – such as not taking part in the annual price-fixing in the Agriculture Council. He thanked me for the papers which, he said, were very clear. He paused and then went on. 'They tell me that you really care about Europe.' I said that I did. He said: 'Well, that's all right by me. But just remember that I really care about the Labour Party.' I took this to mean that, contrary to some expectations, the renegotiation and the Referendum promised by it were designed by Mr Wilson and Mr Callaghan to keep us in the Community, not to take us out. Their decisions in the coming weeks confirmed this interpretation. And so I helped them with zeal. The two-to-one vote to stay in the Community in May 1975 meant a great deal to me.

From 1976 to 1979, as the Deputy Under-Secretary in charge of Economic Affairs, I was not quite so directly and continuously involved. But I still went with Mr Callaghan (now Prime Minister) to meetings of the European Council three times a year and was often engaged in discussion of policy in London. Soon after Mrs Thatcher entered Downing Street in 1979, I was offered the job of Permanent Representative in Brussels, and arrived there on Guy Fawkes' Day, 5 November 1979, just as the first major battles of the British budget campaign were beginning.

A hundred times in the last six years, as I crawled out of bed at dawn to take a plane or into bed at dawn after a late-night Council meeting or when things turned out badly wrong in the Council at two in the morning, my wife or staff have heard me growl: 'I *hate* the Community!' It is hard for those who practise Europe to love it. But, despite the irritation it has often caused me, I still really care about it.

There are many different strands in this European conviction. Most of them will emerge from the substantive chapters of this book. There is the fact that medium-sized countries like Britain, France or Germany do not carry sufficient weight in the modern world to protect and promote their interests. There is the trend, as the world gets smaller due to modern communications, for most countries to become members of a regional organisation. The European Community is ours and we need to be members of it. There are many things we need to do together in Europe – to create a single great market; to cooperate to beat off the American and Japanese bids for supremacy in high technology and other industries; to share our research efforts; to take common action on the environment; to create a zone of monetary stability; even to organise our agricultural and fishing industries; to name only a few.

We have also to think about what things would be like if there were no Community, or if there was and Britain were not a member of it. It is the Community, with its probably irreversible process of integration leading to more integration, which provides us with an absolute assurance that France, Britain and Germany will never fight each other again. What an achievement that is, forty years after 1945! It is the Community which during the last decade of inflation/recession has, time and time again, checked the tendency in Western Europe for countries to go it alone, to protect their industries, to try to export their unemployment by cutting back on their imports from their neighbours, to resort to competitive devaluations, in short to return to the worst forms of economic nationalism of the interwar years. If the Community did not exist we should have to try to invent it. But I do not see the present-day Jean Monnets to help us.

To sit outside a Community which was making its way would not be so catastrophic as it would be not to have it at all. But it would be uncomfortable, unconstructive and enfeebling; uncomfortable because we should have in practice little choice but to conform to many decisions taken in its Councils without having a say in what they should be, as the EFTA countries are finding; unconstructive because what happens in the Community will to a large extent determine what Europe is like in the mid-21st century and those who are outside cannot play a fully constructive role, even if they can restrain themselves from being destructive; and ultimately enfeebling because a country which does not join in building up the unity of Western Europe in the world and the internal unity of the single great market will have no international influence, and its industries and services will have to concentrate on finding niches for themselves on the periphery.

I have heard many sensible people complaining about the Community these last thirteen years. Complaints about the Community are not all wrong. It has its warts, such as the agricultural surpluses. But glorious isolation is not an option in this shrinking world. We have nowhere else to go. Where there are things wrong with the Community, we must work to put them right; where there are things right with the Community, we must give it due credit.

Finally, let it not be forgotten that for Jean Monnet and his friends the Community idea was a means of allowing ancient nation states to merge in a common enterprise and yet to give full play, for as long as their peoples want it, to their individual traditions and diversity. The idea is working. That is no mean achievement and the historians in the 22nd century may say that it was the principal contribution to the welfare of nations which Western Europe made in the second half of the 20th century.

I have declared my interest. I do not conceal that I want the reader to draw the conclusion that it is important for the Community, and for Britain in it, to succeed. But this book is an attempt to describe it objectively as it is. When Nicolas Thompson of Heinemann suggested to me that I should write it, my first reaction was that it was an impossible task to describe the Community without boring everyone to tears. My first reaction may have been right. But my second reaction was that the impossible task ought to be attempted in order to help, even if only in a small way, to fill the gap in public information. How can people judge the Community fairly if those who know it do not take the trouble to try to inform them? The book is not, of course, a comprehensive and detailed picture of all the things which the Community does. You would need twenty books for that. It is a photograph of what the Community was at the beginning of 1986 and the way it works and of how it relates to national politics and government, highlighting the things which seem to me to be important. It is not a learned tome. It is almost entirely written from memory and I am acutely aware how memories differ. I seek indulgence if the memories of others are not the same or if I have got a detail wrong here or there. I have tried to tell the truth as I see it.

When this book appears, it will be nearly a year after my retirement and half a year after I finished it. Things will have happened in many of the fields of activity discussed in it. I hope and believe that I have kept up with events, but the book has to be a little less than a hundred per cent up to date. On the other hand, the way the Community works changes very slowly indeed and the picture of its decision-taking processes that I paint is likely to remain a reasonable likeness well into the next decade. My hope is that it will help the reader to understand the Community's mysterious processes better.

Finally, I should say – though I doubt if anyone would think the contrary – that the book has been written without the benefit of access to official records and that the opinions expressed in it are entirely my own.

1

What is the European Community?

No ONE KNOWS everything about what is going on in the Community. Certainly I don't. This was, for example, forcibly impressed on me when, one day in July 1985, I heard Mr John MacGregor, then Minister of State in the Ministry of Agriculture, briefing the European Democratic Group – mainly the Conservative members of the European Parliament – about the present state of the Common Agricultural Policy. The MEPs were asking him a string of well-informed and detailed questions, clearly matters about which their constituents were deeply concerned, and Mr MacGregor was answering these questions with an impressive assurance. Although I have been following the main developments in the Common Agricultural Policy closely for fifteen years, I did not normally get involved in the detailed negotiations in the Agriculture Council and therefore did not have in my head the details of the operation of the Milk Quota Scheme, the Commission's latest views on oilseed rape, or how the arrangements for 'clawback' on exports of lamb are working.

Even well-informed readers of the *Financial Times*, which has the best coverage on European Community matters of any paper in the world and is read by those who matter in Brussels, have probably only a hazy idea about what the Community does and does not do or how it works or about the different functions of the Commission and the Council. They are in good company. Ignorance prevails on high as well as at the grass-roots. After attending thirty-four meetings of the Heads of Government of the Community – The European Council, as it has been called since 1974 – it is clear to me that some of them, especially in their first year, often do not have a clear idea of how things work. This is understandable, given the complications. The Heads of Government no doubt all receive a pile of briefs several inches thick before each meeting. Even Mrs Thatcher, always reading when others sleep, complains that hers, compressed as much as possible by her Civil Servants, are unreadably long.

At the other end of the scale from Heads of Government, let us take the example of the individual milk producer whose whole livelihood is directly affected by the decisions of the Commission and the Council. Even on their own subject they seem to have suffered from a lack of information before the introduction of milk quotas. At any rate, they complained vigorously that they had been taken by surprise. Yet the Commission had initially proposed a system of quotas – 'guarantee thresholds' in the jargon – in the summer of 1981. The UK supported the Commission's proposal, but there were still too many member governments against. In 1982 and 1983, the debate went on as milk production continued rising.

More governments came out in favour of quotas in the autumn of 1983 and this was one of the subjects dealt with at length, but not settled, at the European Council in Athens in December. The Commission formally proposed quotas early in 1984 as part of its published proposals for the annual price-fixing. It is distressing that, in such circumstances, small producers should have suffered serious losses because they were unprepared when the decision was taken in March 1984.

Ignorance is not the only problem. Unfortunately, many of the things which people do 'know' about the Community are myths. It is, for example, a myth that the Commission is a huge, faceless and idle bureaucracy. On the contrary, compared with most national ministries in any of the member states or even with the Wandsworth Borough Council, it is a small and dedicated body of men and women, many of whom are, of course, interpreters and translators, since the Community has to operate in all its languages. To say this is not to deny that pockets of underemployment exist in it and that sometimes its proposals contain imperfections!

It is also a myth, perpetuated by the popular press, that the Commission only has to propose something for it to be decided. For example, in the late seventies, the Jenkins Commission put forward proposals for Community rules about worker-participation in company decisions, known after the then Commissioner responsible for Social Affairs, Mr Vredeling. The Council has not adopted those proposals and is highly unlikely ever to do so. Yet they have loomed large in the minds of British employers ever since. Mrs Thatcher came to power and firmly rejected them. British ministers and officials explained to anxious company chairmen that there was no risk of them being adopted. The climate of opinion in the Community changed, and the risk of strong pressure building up in favour of the Vredeling proposals faded. But companies were still lobbying the political groups in the European Parliament. The briefs prepared for company chairmen and other directors visiting Brussels still always drew attention to the allegedly serious risk that the British Government

11

would cave in and accept the proposals as part of some package deal. I have had to explain several hundred times that this risk was not to be taken seriously. I am not complaining. It is the job of the Permanent Representative to explain to visiting businessmen what is happening and what is not .

But company time and money were being spent to no purpose. Other far more important and immediate decisions of interest to company chairmen were under discussion in Brussels! Many companies are not organized to follow Community work even on matters such as the steps needing to be taken in order to complete the Common Market, by doing away with the remaining non-tariff barriers in their field by 1992, or draft regulations which the Commission is working on in order to protect the environment. They often have a priority need, which they do not know they have, to be informed in good time so that they can lobby the Commission effectively *before* it puts forward formal proposals.

It is not only businesses which ought to know more. Most citizens now need to know something about what is going on in the Community. Yet how many people know that JET, the laboratory at Culham near Oxford, which is working on the possibility of using fusion rather than fission as a main source of energy in the twenty-first century, is a Community project? How many people know that the Coal and Steel Community Treaty, still in force, gave the Commission, with the assent of the Council, the power to declare a state of 'manifest crisis' in the European steel industry, as they had to do in 1978, and that it was on this basis that Vice-President Davignon was able, again with the consenting opinion of the Council, to fix steel prices and lay down production quotas, negotiate steel plant closures, and limit imports into the Community, thus preserving the European steel industry from even worse disasters in the early eighties? Do all those who ought to do so know that it is the Commission, in accordance with a mandate given by the Council, which has the responsibility for negotiating in the GATT on the future of the Multi-Fibre arrangement which will have a crucial influence on the future of the European textile industry? That the Commission has to be notified of national state aids to industry and to approve them? That the European Court of Luxembourg, the Supreme Court of the Community as far as Community Law is concerned, is something quite different from the European Court of Human Rights in Strasbourg, a body which has been causing the British government some trouble lately and has nothing whatever to do with the European Community?

THE INSTITUTIONS

The first thing to do in order to paint a picture of Community life seems to be to describe the institutions of the Community, rather than the subjects they usually deal with. (We speak about *the* European Community, though, strictly speaking, there are still three, the ECSC, Euratom, and the EEC. Their executives were merged in the European Commission in 1965, but not their treaties.) The institutions of the Community were designed by Jean Monnet and his friends and colleagues in and out of the governments of France, Germany, Italy and Benelux as a framework for sharing sovereignty by consent and for creating an irreversible movement towards ever-greater European integration. The structure is unique in human political and economic organisation, and there is no word in the textbooks on political theory to describe it.

The Community is far from being a federation with a directly-elected central government, despite its directly-elected Parliament. Yet it is far beyond the stage of inter-governmental cooperation between sovereign states. The states have already given up most of their sovereignty in some fields (e.g. state aids and competition), partially shared it in varying degrees in others, and will without doubt share much more in the years immediately ahead. Incidentally, it is wrong to think of sovereignty as a precious commodity to be hoarded at all costs. There is little you can do with it if you keep it. If you share it, you may solve a real problem.

Of course, the Community is not unique as far as sharing sovereignty is concerned. Membership of NATO, for example, involves it too, on a big scale. But it is unique in making laws, directly applicable in all its member States, with a Supreme Court to 'ensure that they are observed'. Where there is a conflict between national and Community law the nation's own courts, and the European Court in the last resort, have the duty under the Treaty, enshrined in British law by the European Community Act of 1972, of ensuring that European law prevails.

The Community is, however, above all unique, as I hope this book will show, in possessing institutions which through their interaction with each other ensure that there is a balance (not always perfect, of course) between the national and the Community interest as the Community gradually increases its role in the national life; and they work, as they were designed to work, to make the process of increasing integration continual if not even. Friends of the Community are prone to say that Britain has never understood it. That may be true, but is probably equally true in varying degrees of other member states. It would probably surprise the French and Germans almost as much as the British themselves to know the extent to which all their countries have already travelled down the road to 'the ever-closer union' which the Treaty of Rome's first sentence lays down as its aim.

Once a subject is given to the institutions of the Community to deal with, it is extremely difficult for the member states, even if they all agree, to get it out again. The Treaty itself put a fair part of the national life within the Community domain and, under Article 235, new subjects such as the environment can be, and regularly have been, added where Community action is necessary to attain one of its objectives (which are widely drawn). The amendments to the Treaty agreed in Luxembourg in December 1985 have added substantially to the activities specifically covered by the Treaty, e.g. the Regional Fund, Research and Technological Development, the Environment.

Once the competence of the Community is established, in the sense that the Community has adopted internal rules on a subject, those rules come under the jurisdiction of the European Court and are no longer matters on which the member states are free each to lay down their own rules or to negotiate separately with other countries. The treaties which set up the institutions and the institutions themselves are designed not only to deal effectively with complex subjects and to promote common policies, to set up the Customs Union or to run the Common Commercial Policy, but also to promote 'ever-closer union'.

The four main institutions are the Commission, the Parliament, the Court and, especially, the Council. There are others, such as the Economic and Social Committee, in which representatives of the employers and workers meet and work out opinions for the Commission and the Council on proposed legislation; the European Investment Bank, which borrows on the market and lends both within the Community and for projects in associated countries; or the Court of Auditors, which reports on whether the Community's money is well spent. But it is the four central institutions which make the Community unique.

THE COMMISSION

The Commission is a major innovation in international life. It is the guardian of the treaties and has the responsibility of taking national governments before the Court if they seem to be in breach of Community law. It has important powers of its own, for example, to enforce the rules of competition, if necessary by imposing substantial fines on those who do not comply. It has the power and the duty to take the initiative and to make new proposals for common policies as well as being responsible under the Council for the implementation of existing policies. The Treaty provides that in many areas there has to be a

Commission proposal before there is a Council decision. Even where this is not the case, very little happens in the Community without it. People have tended to allege in recent years that the Commission was in decline. But that is not my own observation. Even the Thorn Commission (1981–85) played a crucial role on many subjects, having some extremely effective Commissioners, especially Davignon (the dynamic Belgian Commissioner in charge of all industrial and research matters and with great influence on much else besides), though it was a weak Commission as a collegiate body. The Delors Commission (1985–), under his effective and determined leadership, has already raised it several notches in the scale of power and influence.

Before Spain and Portugal joined, there were fourteen Commissioners, two each from the four bigger member states, France, Germany, Britain and Italy, and one each from the other six, the Netherlands, Belgium, Luxembourg, Denmark, Ireland, and Greece. Fourteen is quite enough to carry the present burden of work and it is a well-known phenomenon that it becomes twice as difficult for a chairman to get his committee to have a collegiate sense for every member added beyond ten or twelve. The British Government therefore proposed that, after Spain and Portugal joined on 1st January 1986, the bigger member countries (including Spain) should give up their second Commissioner and each country should have one, i.e. there would have been a total of twelve. This is a good idea whose time does not yet seem to have come. There are now seventeen Commissioners with two Spaniards and one Portuguese.

The Commission is appointed by a common accord between the member governments for four years and its President for two, though he is usually reappointed for another two and Commissioners quite often have two or three terms, remaining in office for eight or twelve years or even longer. I do not remember a case when one member government has objected to another's nomination. It has been proposed that the President-elect should have a say about who his colleagues should be, which is another good idea whose time may not yet have come. Mr Roy Jenkins tried to influence Chancellor Schmidt in this way in 1976, but was unsuccessful, and there has never been effective backing from the governments, even for the principle.

Once they are appointed, Commissioners have to forswear taking instructions from the governments of the countries from which they come and, incidentally, cannot be sacked by those governments. They do not represent their countries in the Community – this is the task of the Ministers in the Council and of the Permanent Representatives on a day-to-day basis. But they are expected to keep in touch with their own countries and governments, to know what is going on there and how Commission proposals under discussion are likely to be received. If they have influence with their own governments, they are more useful to the Commission. No one is surprised if a Commissioner refers to the difficulties which would be caused by a given proposal in 'the member country he knows best'. On the other hand, a Commissioner will be much criticized if he is believed to be taking instructions from the government of that country, intervening unscrupulously to promote its interests, or trying to get that government to intervene in the affairs of the Commission.

Under the Commissioners, the Directors-General and the Commission staff are, with a few exceptions, career officials who have worked for the Community for many years. The most senior of them all is the Secretary-General, Emile Noel, who has held the job since the beginning. Now nearing retirement, he has played a key role in every major event of the last twenty-eight years. He takes the minutes of the Commission as well as being the President's principal adviser on appointments, rather like the Secretary of the Cabinet in Whitehall. Wise and calm, a tireless worker, he always appears at the right moment to protect the Community interest and often to suggest an imaginative solution to an intractable problem.

Occasionally at very senior level, an official from a member state is appointed to take the place of one of his compatriots who is retiring or resigning. There are conflicting principles involved here. On the one hand, it is part of the accepted doctrine that there should be a broad geographical balance and that officials from each country should, as far as possible, be present in all parts of the Commission and should overall be present in numbers roughly related to the importance of the countries concerned. So if, for example, an Italian in an important post resigns, the Italian Government may be keen to see him replaced by another Italian, either by promotion within the Commission or, if not, by 'parachuting' from outside. On the other hand, the Commission rightly defends strongly the principle that able people should be encouraged to make their whole career there, with reasonable prospects of promotion, a principle to which the staff themselves naturally attach paramount importance. So there are strong pressures in favour of internal promotion, against 'parachuting' and against attaching national labels to particular jobs.

In theory at least, the Commission officials should be even more independent of their national governments and impartial than Commissioners themselves. In practice, performance varies. Commission officials, as well as Commissioners themselves, keep in close touch with the governments, and especially the Permanent Representatives and their staffs, from their own countries. It is right that they should do so if they are to be able to keep the Commission informed and to play a part in persuading those governments to accept Commission proposals. But they have constantly to bear in mind that they will reduce their own capacity for influence in the Commission if they are seen to be paying too much attention to the views of those governments. Equally, the national governments need to learn the lesson that they cannot expect their Commissioners or officials always to do what they would like and that it is counter-productive to be seen to be putting too much pressure on them. A wise Permanent Representative does well to ensure that his government gets its way as often as possible by lobbying Commissioners from other countries than his own.

Political alignment plays a role. For example, the British have traditionally appointed a Senior Commissioner (the big countries having two) from the party in power – Christopher Soames (1973–77), Roy Jenkins (1977–81), Christopher Tugendhat (1981–85), and Arthur Cockfield (1985–), while the second job has gone to the Opposition, George Thomson (1973–77), Christopher Tugendhat (1977–81), Ivor Richard (1981–85) and Stanley Clinton Davies (1985–). Where the two main parties in the UK are divided on an issue arising in Commission discussions, it is only natural that conviction as well as interest should often push the senior Commissioner in the direction of the government which appointed him – and vice versa. To say this is not to accuse the senior British Commissioners of constantly toeing the government line or the second Commissioners of always putting national political games above their duty to the European interest. Neither is true and the British may even be less susceptible to home political pressures than some of their Continental colleagues. But the point needs to be made in order to bring out how intensely political Community life is.

On the other hand, the extent to which Commissioners have lined up in Commission debates on party political lines has been limited. Of course, Christian Democrat or Socialist Commissioners are likely to be more closely in touch with the group of their own persuasion in the European Parliament; and there are issues on which a Left/Right division can arise within the Commission. But, so far, and seen from the outside, this has not seemed to be a major factor determining the Commission's course. It is interesting, in fact, that some of the most effective Commissioners, at least in my time, have moved to the Commission from being senior officials in their own governments – Gundelach of Denmark, for example, and Davignon himself.

Each Commissioner has to work out for himself how far to go in the direction either of independence or of following the wishes of his government. Permanent Representatives are often the pig-in-the-middle. They have to spend as much time explaining to their governments why 'their' Commissioners are unable or unwilling to do exactly what the government wants as they do trying to persuade the Commissioner concerned to make as much as possible of their government's views his own. For the Commissioners have many reasons to go their own European way.

They see a great deal of each other, and in a good Commission there are strong pressures in the direction of collegiate action. The Commission offices are mainly in a large modern glass building with four wings and a concave front, close to the centre of Brussels, called the Berlaymont. The Commissioners all work on the thirteenth floor and there they have their weekly meetings, almost always on Wednesdays, though they sometimes meet on other days as well. There is a premium on good preparation of Commission meetings. Each Commissioner has a 'cabinet', larger and more powerful than the Private Office of a Minister in the British Government, but still only six to eight people. The Chefs de Cabinet meet on Mondays to prepare the Commission and much telephoning and tramping the corridors of the thirteenth floor by members of the cabinet and by Commissioners themselves has to take place on Tuesday if a Commissioner attaches importance to getting his way on a given item on Wednesday. Alliances have to be made, favours returned or extended, concessions made in pre-negotiation. With a strong President, it is vital to get him on your side. (It is not so very different from the way a national government works.) If necessary, decisions are taken by majority vote. But a good President likes to be able to say that on important matters the Commission is solidly behind him and so votes do not take place at every meeting.

It is the Commission which puts forward draft Community legislation, and this is sent to the Parliament for an opinion before the Council can take a decision. The Commission is always present in the Council and an able Commissioner can often have more influence on the outcome of the Council's decisions than even the President of the Council and certainly than any of its members. To see Davignon (1977–85) persuading, bullying, cajoling, wheeling and dealing in the Council and emerging with agreed conclusions on the lines he wanted all along was a pure delight and a living denial of the thesis that the Commission is powerless or purely technocratic.

Davignon, moreover, demonstrated, if demonstration was required, that a Commissioner need not come from one of the bigger countries to have a major influence. In the Thorn Commission, he had more influence than any two or three other Commissioners put together. This is a fairly conclusive answer to those who say that the bigger countries need two Commissioners to reflect their weight and importance. One good Commissioner should be enough to explain his country's economic and political problems to his colleagues.

THE EUROPEAN COURT

I deal next with the Court because Community law is the second major innovation in the Community's structure. Under the Treaty it is directly applicable in all the member states – that is to say, a citizen or a company in France or Britain can go to a French or British court for a ruling against another citizen or company, or against the national government itself, in accordance with Community legislation. If the national court is in doubt about the proper interpretation of Community law it refers the matter to the European Court in Luxembourg. If there is a conflict between a national law and a Community law, the latter prevails.

More frequently, however, matters are referred to the Court by the Commission or, occasionally, by member governments. When the Commission, as the guardian of the Treaties, considers that there is *prima facie* evidence of a breach of Community Law by a member government or that a member government has not taken proper action to enforce Community law when adopted, it first seeks an explanation from that government. If it is not satisfied with the explanation, it refers the matter to the European Court for a judgement which is final. Equally, a member state may go to the Court to test the legality of the actions of the Commission or another member government. And finally, the European Parliament has now created a precedent by successfully taking the Council itself to the Court for breach of its obligation under the EEC Treaty to introduce a Common Transport Policy.

The Court has as yet no means of imposing sanctions on a rebellious member government. But it is significant that no member government has ever failed to obey the Court's rulings for long, though several have been slow about it, for example the French over the British lamb imports. The member States who are taken before the Court most often for alleged infractions of Community law have been France and Italy.

The workload of the Court is heavy and growing. The cases before it are often extremely complicated and break new ground. So its judgements frequently take a year or more. If however it considers that the risk of damage being done meanwhile justifies it, the Court may decide on 'interim measures' which can have the effect of an injunction from a British court.

The Court is now composed of twelve Judges and six Advocates-General. The latter prepare the cases. The Judges, under their President, Lord Mackenzie–Stuart (originally from the Edinburgh bar) sit as a whole and by mysterious processes not known to outsiders succeed during the course of their deliberations in reaching an agreed judgement.

In the Community, as in other human institutions, personal relations play their part. A Commissioner or Ambassador, like anyone else, will take more trouble for a friend than for someone he does not know. The Community lends itself to lobbying and Commissioners, Parliamentarians, Ministers and even Permanent Representatives are constantly on the receiving end. But the Judges are, rightly, very careful not to expose themselves to this sort of thing. Though Lord Mackenzie-Stuart and his wife were friends of ours before the European Community was invented, I always had to be careful, in private conversations with him, to avoid mentioning any particular case before the Court. It would be quite wrong for any Representative of a government to try to influence such cases, except through the formal procedures laid down. I have not come across examples of this principle being breached.

With every year that passes and with new subjects being dealt with each year by the institutions of the Community, the proportion of Community law relative to national law is growing in all member states. In addition, the Court's judgements, rather naturally, tend in the direction of strengthening the role of Community law.

Recent events in the fields of insurance and aviation demonstrate the importance of the Court as a prime mover in breaking down the remaining barriers in the Community. If it becomes possible in the 1990s to write insurance polices in Germany out of London, if air fares in Europe come down to the price per mile prevalent in the U.S. (say, a third of that in Europe), it will, to a large extent, be due to the decisions of the European Court in 1986 to enforce the Treaty of Rome in these fields.

Though there are differences, an analogy can be drawn between the role of the Court and that of the Supreme Court in the United States. Both have the task of interpreting a written Constitution, the Treaties (of ECSC, Euratom and EEC in the case of the Community), as well as being the final Court of Appeal about what is the current law. The main difference is that, as becomes a federation, the Supreme Court has jurisdiction over the whole of American law, whereas the European Court has no jurisdiction over the laws of the member states unless they conflict with the growing body of Community law.

THE PARLIAMENT

Under the Treaty, the Parliament was at first appointed from among the members of the national Parliaments, but provision was made for it eventually to be directly elected. In 1974, President Giscard proposed, and the other Heads of Government agreed, that this provision should be implemented.

With some difficulty, an agreement between the member states on how direct elections should be arranged was drawn up and the first ones took place throughout the Community in 1979. The Parliament has a five–year term, and the second direct elections duly took place in 1984.

Each member state has a quota of Members of the European Parliament. The bigger countries naturally have more, but not in a direct relation to population, the smaller member states, particularly Luxembourg, having a greater representation. So far it has not been possible to agree on a common electoral system (as foreseen in Article 138 of the Treaty), the British being the most important obstacle owing to the unwillingness of either the Labour or Conservative Governments to adopt any form of proportional representation. So each country uses its own or something very like its own electoral system, Britain (except for Northern Ireland) its first-past-the-post winner system with very large individual constituences (on average eight national constituencies).

The Parliament meets in Strasbourg in plenary session for the inside of a week each month except August. In two out of three other weeks, each month, its Committees meet in Brussels.

In the Parliament, the various parties band together in trans-national groups of which the two most important are the Christian Democrats and the Socialists, followed by the Liberals, the 'European Democratic Group' (originally the British Conservatives with one or two Danes, and now enlarged by the addition of eighteen representatives of the Spanish right-of-centre party, the Popular Alliance) the Communists, the French Gaullists and so on. The British Labour members sit in the Socialist group, but many of them hold very different views from the rest of their Socialist colleagues, who are shocked by those who express openly anti-Market views. In the Chamber, members sit in a hemi-cycle facing the President, with the Communists on the left and the right-wing parties on the right. These groups are not as tightly disciplined as in most national Parliaments, but nevertheless, the general tendency is for members of the groups to vote the same way much of the time.

The powers of the European Parliament reflect the unique structure of the Community somewhere between a federation and inter-governmental co-operation. There is no central government to be responsible to the Parliament which is therefore, to its members' frustration, not like national Parliaments in Europe in this (and other) crucial respects. Because there is no government majority in Parliament, with ministers constantly explaining their policies and trying to keep their supporters in line, it is difficult for MEPs to address themselves to draft legislation in a practical and responsible way. Furthermore, Community legislation has to be fitted in with national legislation and the governments therefore, when they wrote the Treaties, reserved to the Council the final say about legislation. In sharp contrast to the roles of parliament and government in, say, the UK, the Parliament is not the legislature. It has to give an opinion on the Commission's proposals for draft legislation and will in future (if the Treaty amendments agreed in Luxembourg in December 1985 are ratified by all the national parliaments) be able to *propose* amendments to them. But it is the Council, that is to say the governments acting collectively, which rejects, redrafts or approves proposals for legislation.

There is a strong movement in the Parliament, naturally enough, for additional powers to be given to it and this is reflected in some sections of public opinion, especially in Italy and Germany. There has been talk of a 'democratic deficit' needing to be remedied. But it has to be remembered that it is the Council that takes the decisions and ministers acting in the Council are responsible to their own national parliaments. Most ministers do not favour any important transfer of powers to the Parliament at the present stage of its development and it seems likely that it will have to content itself with, broadly speaking, the powers that it now has and the increasing influence that they can give it for the next decade or two. (I shall come back to this issue in Chapter 12 when discussing possible constitutional change.)

An important power which it has not yet used is its ability to sack the Commission. But talk of using it has been increasing since the first direct elections and this has had a considerable effect on both the Thorn and Delors Commissions, who naturally, for both political and personal reasons, wish to avoid that fate. As a result, the Commission pays a great deal of attention to the views of the Parliament in its preparation of draft legislation, in the line it takes in the Council when the moment of decision is approaching and in budgetary matters (where the Parliament and the Council, with slightly different roles and powers, share the responsibility for decisions).

The threat to sack the Commission may not be quite as real as some in the Commission fear. It will not be easy to get the requisite majority in the Parliament, whose members are acutely aware that they would need to carry public opinion in the member states with them. Since it is the member governments that appoint the Commission, there would be a real risk of the Parliament being made to look foolish if the member governments regarded its action as unreasonable and reappointed virtually the same members.

The Parliament's other main power is to approve or reject the annual budget. A draft budget is proposed by the Commission, usually in May, and amended by the Council and sent to the Parliament in July. In the autumn, the Council and the Parliament, the two halves of the budgetary authority, engage in a process of negotiation. In December, the Council sends a final draft to the Parliament. On two occasions the Parliament has rejected it (1981 and 1984). But on neither occasion did the Parliament manage to wring substantial concessions out of the Council before the pressure of events and public opinion forced it to approve an only slightly revised version.

In several other recent years, the Parliament have made significant changes (more important in the 1985 debate on the 1986 budget than in previous years) which the Council did not accept, and the President of the Parliament has signed it in that form. So far the Commission have shown themselves ready to implement the Parliament's version; and, until this year, the Council have not carried its objections to the point of pressing a Court case to a decision. At the time of going to press, it begins to look as though the Court will give a judgement in 1986.

I should add that there is a distinction between 'obligatory' and 'non-obligatory' expenditure, the former being expenditure directly flowing from obligations entered into under the Community's policies and comprising the vast majority of CAP expenditure. The Parliament's influence on this part of the budget is therefore less, though it can, of course, reject the budget as a whole if it does not like the Council's decisions on obligatory expenditure.

The disputes between the Council and the Parliament are legally and substantively extremely complicated. They have arisen mainly from two causes. First, the amendments to Article 203 of the Treaty agreed in 1975 (under the Labour Government and just after the referendum) left a certain ambiguity about the extent to which the Parliament has the last word on non- obligatory expenditure. Secondly, the provisions about the permitted rate of increase of non-obligatory expenditure, the 'maximum rate', are also liable to give rise to differences of interpretation. The maximum rate is calculated according to a formula which takes account of GNP growth, average growth in national budgets and inflation in the previous year. The Parliament is permitted to increase the budget by half the maximum rate, even if the Council has already used up more than half of it, and the two institutions together may increase the maximum rate itself if they agree. Since the distinction between obligatory and non-obligatory expenditure is itself the subject of controversy, it is not surprising that disputes arise – though it would in my view be difficult to find legal arguments to justify the Parliament's action in regard to the 1986 budget.

These disputes are bad for the Community. They show how dangerous it is to try to give the Parliament minor satisfaction by ambiguous language, as was done in 1975. Personally, I favoured trying to put this mistake right in the Treaty revision exercise of 1985, even if that meant giving the Parliament some small additional dissatisfaction, by making it unambiguously clear that both the Council and the Parliament, the two halves of the budgetary authority, had to put their names to the budget before it could be adopted. I still think it was a pity that other governments were reluctant to grasp this nettle.

It is hard to assess the extent to which the Parliament's unchanged budgetary powers can be exploited. They have certainly already brought the Parliament into the calculations of the Council as an important factor in Community affairs. Indeed, it is clear that, over the past six years since direct elections, the Parliament has considerably increased its role and will no doubt continue to do so. But, as seen from the Council, the fact that the Parliament has no power to block the provision of finance, only to increase it marginally, the relative incoherence of the positions the Parliament takes in its resolutions and the difficulty of fashioning it into an effective bargaining instrument with the Council will make it hard for the Parliament to extract from the member governments and national parliaments the increases in its own powers and influence which it seeks.

Up to now, the European Parliament has always wanted to spend more money than the Council. There is no reason to think that this will change. MEPs can use Community expenditure in their constituencies – or even countries – in their electoral addresses. More Community expenditure means marginally more weight for the Community budget in relation to national budgets; and European Parliamentarians, like Commissioners and even Judges, are normally on the side of those who want the Community gradually to play a bigger role.

Parliamentarians, in particular, feel a strong need for this. To say the least, elections to the European Parliament, which do not determine the political colour of the Community's government, do not arouse the same interest as national elections either. Many feel that a low turn-out reflects badly on the Community and diminishes their prestige and influence. They feel that the answer must be to increase the powers and the role of the Parliament and thus the public interest in its elections. Since that solution will not be adopted in the near future, it is hard to see what can be done. Perhaps direct elections came too soon. But the decision, like so much else in the Community, is irreversible and the elected Parliament has enlivened the Community's life. Perhaps the Parliament will have to live with low turn-outs in its elections for the rest of the century – and even beyond.

THE COUNCIL

Finally I come to the Council which is the main decision-taking body and, of course, the institution I know best. Under the Treaty, there is only one Council, assisted by a Secretary-General and a secretariat and composed of Ministers from each of the member states together with a Commissioner. In practice, Ministers in charge of many different departments in national governments meet in the Council; therefore, though they all naturally have the same constitutional role, people tend to speak of the Agriculture Council or the Environment Council; and indeed, like any other body of people who meet frequently each one takes on a slightly different personality.

The Foreign Ministers' Council which meets every month except August (and sometimes more often) is also known as the General Affairs Council. It not only deals with the external affairs of the Community but with a number of key issues such as constitutional questions, the British budget problem, regional policy, and so on. It has responsibility for co-ordinating the work of the Community on important questions and preparing the meetings of the European Council (of Heads of Government) which Foreign Ministers also attend.

Decisions on the CAP are taken by the Council of Agriculture Ministers. It too meets every month and considerably more often in March, April and sometimes May, when its main decisions (on the annual price-fixing) are taken. It treats matters of considerable detail and most of the time leads a life of its own, prepared by its own group of senior officials, the Special Committee on Agriculture.

In addition, a large number of other ministers meet in Council, such as Finance, Budget, Development (i.e. aid to the Third World), Research, Energy, Transport, Industry/Steel, Environment, Social Affairs, and Education Ministers.

These councils have slightly different roles depending on whether they are co-ordinating national policies (Finance Ministers on economic policy), taking decisions on day-to-day matters (Industry Ministers on steel), or adopting Community legislation (Environment Ministers on exhaust emissions).

The Treaty lays down that certain matters shall be decided by unanimity, others by qualified majority voting with member states having a weighted number of votes related to their size (though the smaller member states are privileged in comparison with the size of their population), or by a simple majority for procedural matters. I shall deal in later chapters with the controversial question of how the majority voting provisions actually work,

25

and the so-called Luxembourg Compromise of 1966, under which certain member states hold that votes should not take place on matters of very important national interest against the wishes of the member state concerned.

On some matters, the Council can decide without a formal proposal by the Commission and quite frequently does so, for example, on matters affecting relations with other countries. Often, however, the Treaty lays down that there must be a formal proposal. As far as draft legislation is concerned, there has not only to be a formal proposal, but an opinion by the European Parliament before the Council can take a decision. Even where majority voting applies, unanimity is required to amend a Commission proposal, unless of course the Commission decides to amend it itself. These provisions add to the influence of the Commission in the Council.

Each six months, on January 1st and July 1st, the Presidency of the Council and of all its subordinate bodies, changes, rotating in alphabetical order among the member states. The Presidency has a major role. In consultation with the Commission and the Secretary-General of the Council, it organises the business of the Community, decides when meetings shall be held and has an important influence on the agenda and the conduct and outcome of the discussions. It is almost impossible to get a decision out of a Council against the wishes of its President. The Presidency also has major functions as representative of the Council in the European Parliament, to which it reports and whose questions it answers, and as representative of the Community in the world, speaking for it in international discussion and visiting other countries on its behalf. When this book is published, the British will have embarked on their third Presidency (first 1977, second 1981).

The Secretary-General is a key figure, if he chooses, both because he briefs the Presidents of the Council and sits beside them in the meetings, but also because he and his staff have the job of drafting many of the 'compromise texts' which become the basis for the final negotiations in the Council. (In any negotiation you can always gain quite a few of the points you want by influencing the drafting of the final text and so the Secretary-General and his staff are much solicited.) The present incumbent, Niels Ersboll, a former Danish Permanent Representative, does choose to exert influence where possible and thus does much behind the scenes to move the Council towards more rapid decisions.

The six-month Presidency is almost certainly on balance the right solution. Of course, it has the disadvantage that new Ministers and officials have to learn the job and there are occasional changes of priorities. Performance is mixed. One theoretical alternative would be to turn the Secretary-General into a permanent Chairman (as in NATO). But he could not chair all the Councils (two or three often meet on one day) and, however impressive he was, he would be hard put to it to preside effectively over so many different Ministers on so wide a variety of technical subjects. Another theoretical alternative would be for the Commissioner responsible to take the chair. But the Commission is an independent participant in the Council, at times almost its adversary, and has a duty to maintain its own viewpoint. Neither Ministers nor the Commission would feel comfortable with such an arrangement. What is more, the Presidency is responsible for organising the busy work-programme of all the Councils in relation to each other and this burden could not be placed on the President of the Commission, who has too much to do already.

So there is no real alternative to the President being a minister. The advantage of rotation is that, at regular intervals, most of the members of each government become involved in, and committed to, getting the Community's business done. A good Foreign Minister and his colleagues at home (and his Permanent Representative) will plan all the Council's business in advance. The UK, for example, was in touch with their Dutch predecessors about the management of one of the Community's major agenda items, the internal market, during the Benelux and British Presidencies of 1985–87, even before the Dutch had taken the chair in January 1986. With so many complicated subjects under discussion, it is essential to prepare the work well in advance so that the different subjects are ripe for discussion in the Council in a sensible order and at the right time. Governments are increasingly aware of this factor.

The burden of the Presidency is heavy, especially, but not only, for the Foreign Minister and the Permanent Representative; so heavy as to be hard to carry for more than six months at a time. Tenure for a year would not only wear out the key people; it would mean that it only came round every twelve years, with the result that no one would be left in office who had done it before. So, by general consent, the Community leaves it at six months each time the subject is examined in one of the periodical reviews of the effectiveness of the institutions.

The Council normally meets in the Charlemagne building next door to the Commission in Brussels, where the Secretariat also works, except in April, June and October when it meets in Luxembourg. These Luxembourg meetings are the result of a compromise deal made when the ECS, Euratom, and EEC executives were merged in 1965. (The ECSC was in Luxembourg.) They are inconvenient for the vast number of people who have to move down to Luxembourg from Brussels. But they are jealously guarded by the

Luxembourg Government who, having already suffered a blow from the Parliament when it decided no longer to have Plenary meetings there, are determined not to let the Council slide towards Brussels. This is not just a question of prestige. The Luxembourg hotel and restaurant industry would be severely damaged. (There is just as much resistance from France to the idea, advocated by some British MEPs, of moving the Plenary sessions of the Parliament from Strasbourg to Brussels.) Since the issue is one to be decided by common accord, changes are hard to make.

Since 1974, the Heads of Government have met three times a year, once in the capital of each Presidency, and once in Brussels (or Luxembourg according to the month), and these meetings were officially renamed 'the European Council'. Three times a year is once too many and the British government suggested some time ago that it meet only twice, once in each Presidency. This is an idea whose time came at the Luxembourg Council in December 1985. There will in future only be two a year.

The European Council is a hybrid body. Under the agreement in Paris in 1974 which set it up, it can be constituted as a formal Council whenever it wishes, provided that it then carries on business in accordance with normal Community procedures. But normally it does not act as a formal Council, issuing its decisions in the form of conclusions; sometimes conclusions agreed word by word by the Heads of Government themselves, sometimes Presidency conclusions issued on the responsibility of the Prime Minister who is in the Chair. In the latter case, there is usually trouble because not all member states agree and those who do not put down a reservation to say that they are not bound by the Presidency conclusion in question, while others who like them continue to refer to them as though they were sacrosanct.

The European Council is not like ordinary councils in other ways. Only the Foreign Ministers join Heads of Government in the meeting-room itself (not even Permanent Representatives are present) and the numerous advisers hang around in the national offices or the Delegates' Room.

Its role has never been clearly agreed. The original concept was that it should give strategic direction and, to some extent, it does. For example, the main impetus towards completing the internal market was given at the Copenhagen meeting in December 1982. The Stuttgart meeting in June 1983 launched the negotiation which led to the linked agreements on budget discipline, the British budget problem and increasing the revenue available to the Community.

Some people, including British ministers, have been tempted from time to time to try to push this function of strategic direction further and to get the

European Council to lay down priorities among all the subjects on the Community agenda. I doubt if this could ever work. Subjects dealt with in one Council cannot easily be given a priority in relation to subjects dealt with in another. Each member state has different ideas about what should – and should not – be done and what should be done soon and what later. A negotiation about priorities across the board would be time-consuming and probably ineffective since the final compromise language would have to give something to everyone or else be very general. So in my view the European Council will do best to give its strategic direction the form of decisions from time to time to settle this or that problem at its next meeting or to launch an important negotiation or, sometimes, to finish one off.

Other people have sometimes suggested that the idea of creating the European Council was a mistake and that it should be allowed to lapse. This must be wrong. The Prime Ministers are the only ministers in national governments who deal with all the subjects that are being negotiated in the various Councils and they need to be engaged if the Community is to work properly. Only they can exert the necessary authority over their Ministers to get them to settle the really difficult questions.

But it is true that from time to time the existence of the European Council has resulted in delaying decisions by ordinary Council meetings on politically sensitive subjects, in the expectation that these will only be settled by the Heads of Government themselves. In consequence, the European Council has had to deal in considerable detail with matters like the setting up of the European Monetary System, the British budget problem, or integrated Mediterranean programmes. Contrary to this practice, happily not a common one, there is general agreement in principle that the European Council ought not to be a Council of last resort, thus delaying decisions in the ordinary Councils. Alas, in the Community to say that something should in principle not take place comes perilously close to admitting that in practice it will.

Under the Council, the Committee of Permanent Representatives (COREPER) and its subordinate bodies play an important role in the life of the Community. The Permanent Representatives (known for prestige reasons as Ambassadors, although their job in no way resembles that of an Ambassador to a country) live in Brussels and represent their governments in direct dealings with the Commission as well as in COREPER. They are supported by high-calibre officials – in the UK case, one Deputy Secretary, one Under-Secretary and eight Assistant Secretaries of whom nearly two thirds come from the Home Civil Service and only one third from the Diplomatic Service. They, with the Commission, are at the centre of Community life.

There is a tendency indeed in the European Parliament to over-estimate the role of COREPER which is seen as a demon institution with a vocation to block the process of European integration and frustrate the Parliament itself. This is an absurd exaggeration. The Permanent Representatives act under instructions from their Ministers. If they have influence with their Ministers, it is normally used to promote solutions not to prevent them. Insofar as they have a collegiate tendency, it is to try to help the Council to solve problems.

COREPER is divided into two parts – Ambassadors and their Deputies, each dealing with different points of the business of the Council. Both parts meet at least once a week. Their main role is to prepare the meetings of the various Councils. Whether Council meetings go well and solve a lot of problems or decide nothing in a state of chaos and acrimony depends to a considerable extent on these preparations. COREPER itself does not do all the work. A large number of working groups meet under its direction and, usually working on proposals by the Commission, go as far as they can towards reaching agreement between the member states. COREPER carries that process further if it can. Matters which can be fully agreed in COREPER are submitted to the Council for formal approval without discussion as a so-called 'A-point', of which there are a considerable number at every Council. If it cannot reach complete agreement, its job is to submit the outstanding differences between member states to the Council in a comprehensible form, if possible with options which improve the chances of agreement in the Council.

The Ambassadors know each other extremely well and do a lot of business together outside meetings. In their formal discussions, they have of course always to speak to the instructions which they have received from their governments and what they say is reported to governments by their staff in telegrams. But in addition they frequently meet collectively but informally, often over lunch, in order to try to thrash out between them ways in which their ministers might possibly solve difficult problems in the Council. Even if several major differences between member states remain, quite often a solution begins to emerge through the mist at these informal meetings, or at the informal working lunches of ministers which almost always take place on the first day of a Council.

In one sense, COREPER and the Council together are a forum for a permanent negotiation between member governments on a wide range of issues simultaneously. In another, they are the legislature of the Community. In a third, they are the senior board of directors taking many of the day-to-day decisions on its policies. In all these roles their activities are extensively reported in the media and become part of the political debate at home.

2

The Work of the Community

EXTERNAL AND INTERNAL. THE COMMON AGRICULTURAL POLICY

ONE MAJOR PART of the Community's work concerns the relationship with other countries, how best to defend and promote European interests in the world (see Chapter Eleven for further description of this important field of action). Where the Community acts as one as, for example, it is bound to do by the Treaty as far as international trade negotiations are concerned, it carries far more weight than any of the member states individually. It has considerable influence even with the United States. When, for example, the United States Government is considering taking unilateral protectionist measures about steel or wine or shoes, the need to work with the Community or else to face the threat of Community retaliation provides the President and his free-trader advisers with a powerful argument for sticking to the rules of the GATT.

To summarize its international agenda, the Community has free-trade arrangements with the EFTA countries (now Norway, Sweden, Finland, Iceland, Switzerland and Austria) and meets them collectively from time to time. It has bilateral trade and financial co-operation arrangements with most of the countries round and in the Mediterranean. The Lome Convention with well over sixty African, Caribbean and Pacific countries is its key relationship with developing countries, under which the Community provides nearly £1,000 million a year in aid, as well as giving preferential trade access to them. It has a group-to-group relationship with ASEAN, the Andean Pact, and the Central American countries. It has bilateral agreements with countries as diverse as, for example, China, Rumania, India, Canada and Brazil, and gives aid to a number of these 'non-associates' as well as food and emergency aid in the appropriate circumstances. It seeks to adopt common positions in international organizations, particularly in economic ones, such as UNCTAD.

In Political Co-operation, the jargon for co-ordination of foreign policy outside the scope of the Treaties, it also seeks to adopt common positions on many of the important foreign policy issues of the day. The Foreign Ministers often meet with their Political Co-operation hats on, sometimes at the time of Council meetings, sometimes in the capital of the Presidency. In order to prepare these meetings, senior officials from the Foreign Ministries, normally called the Political Directors, meet at least every month in the Political Committee – irreverently known in the Foreign Office as 'Poco' (this is a pity since poco means 'little' in Italian and Spanish, and the British do not intend to belittle political co-operation). Under the Political Directors, senior officials from the various regional departments of the Foreign Ministries also meet frequently to compare notes and to prepare the Political Director's meetings.

There was a time when, at French insistence, an attempt was made to make a rigid distinction between the External Policy of the Community as such and Political Co-operation. On an infamous occasion in 1973, during the first Danish Presidency, M. Jobert (then French Foreign Minister) insisted that Foreign Ministers should meet in Political Co-operation in Copenhagen (the capital of the Presidency) in the morning, and move to Brussels for a Council meeting in the afternoon. Sir Alec Douglas-Home, then Foreign Secretary, took this artificial distinction amiss. I remember him commenting in the plane that Foreign Ministers might wear two hats but they only had one head. He and his colleagues made sure that the French never imposed such an absurdity again.

Indeed, it has since been increasingly recognised that Political Co-operation and the External Policy of the Community are often two sides of the same coin. In regard to Afghanistan, Iran, Poland and Central America, Foreign Ministers have found themselves taking decisions at the same meeting on Council and Political Co-operation business. Following a British initiative in May 1985 agreement was reached by Heads of Government in December 1985 on a treaty formalising the obligation on governments to consult each other on foreign policy generally. A very small but high-powered Secretariat was established, to help the Presidency to run the Political Co-operation machinery. The treaty (when ratified, together with the treaty amendments agreed at the same time) should help to bring the two sides of the external policy of the Community still closer together.

THE INTERNAL AGENDA

The work done to promote the unity of Europe on the world stage is an important part of the Community life. But it is the internal policies which have the biggest political implications in the member states and which are the more complicated. This book can only give a sketchy picture of these internal policies, highlighting a few major questions. The serious student of the Community who wishes to get a more comprehensive summary of the Council's decisions each year can obtain copies of the reports on European Union which the Council makes to the December meeting of the European Council. The Commission also produces a useful, probably more useful, annual report. But if he or she wants to know in detail about any particular policy, the reader will need to resort to specialist publications.

The Community is a new layer of government. Before Community membership, the British people, for example, knew of no authority between Westminster Whitehall and the Almighty. There was no Court of Appeal above the House of Lords. By ratifying the Treaty and passing the European Communities Act, the British Parliament changed all this. Community policies are implemented by Community legislation. The Council adopts the Community's laws, though the member governments have to agree to them. They are not imposed by the Community on member states.

The extent to which the Community is a new layer of Government varies from field to field. In Agriculture, 70% or 80% of the legislation affecting the farming world is Community legislation. In Education, the impact is marginal. For other policies such as Transport or the Environment, the proportion lies in between, the Community part growing.

Those who are against the Community have no doubt in their minds that any Community law is a bad law. Some supporters of the Community seem to take the even more untenable position that any law the Commission proposes must be a good one. Personally I have a strong prejudice against having any more laws, whether Community or national, than are strictly essential in order to deal with the real problems. There were too many laws already, including a few unnecessary Community laws. The criterion for accepting or opposing Community legislation should be whether the thing needs to be done at all and, if it does, whether it is best or necessarily done in the Community rather than nationally.

Mrs Thatcher has been leading a campaign on this subject, with the support of President Delors. Her aim has been to make sure that existing laws are scrutinised to ensure that the burden on enterprise or the citizen does not outweigh the advantages of the action undertaken and to build into the procedure for drafting future legislation an assessment of the regulatory burden.

Sometimes the Community's internal agenda concerns common policies such as fisheries or agriculture, research or the environment. Sometimes it concerns the way the rules are applied; for example, over competition in new high-technology industries or state aids in the steel industry. Sometimes the way Community money is spent on regional or social policy requires discussion. Sometimes the Finance Ministers talk about their macro-economic policies and their impact on each other's countries. At the top of the agenda for the next five years will be the completion of the internal market, making Western Europe into a single great market, almost, but not quite, like the United States market.

In this chapter, I shall deal with the Community's most controversial activity and the one on which more than two-thirds of its budget is spent, the Common Agricultural Policy. Some people think that it occupies an equally major place in the agenda of the Community. This is not so. Only about one eighth of the time of the Council, in all its formations, is taken up by agriculture. Like many other internal policies, but more so than most, the CAP is also a matter of great importance to countries outside the Community and therefore work on it constitutes a significant part of the Community's external policy, as we shall see when we come to Chapter Eleven.

AGRICULTURE

No industrialised country exposes its agriculture to the free play of market forces. To do so would be to subject farmers to the fluctuations of world food prices with which they could not cope and to risk driving many thousands of workers off the land. In countries such as Italy or Greece where a high percentage of the population still work in agriculture, this would be a disaster if done at all quickly and even in the UK, where only 3% do, a development which would be difficult to deal with while unemployment remains so high. In thinking about the CAP you need to keep constantly in mind that for some, like the Germans, it is not primarily the economic but the social effects they mind about. They are prepared to pay heavily to keep small Bavarian farms prosperous. For others, such as Denmark, Ireland, or Greece, it is the main source of net inflows from the Community budget. In most member countries the farm lobby is very powerful, even in the UK.

The main problem about the CAP is that Community farmers are producing ever-growing surpluses – that is to say, in my definition, production in excess of the quantities required for internal consumption (including an appropriate level of stocks to guard against a bad harvest), exports at market prices plus food aid to developing countries. (The farmers' lobby would like to persuade us that subsidized agricultural exports are not really surpluses. This is not a tenable thesis.) How did we come to this?

Part of the original Franco-German deal when the Community was set up was that, in return for freedom for Germany to export its industrial goods within the Community, France should be free to export its agricultural products under a common agricultural policy (CAP). But Article 39 of the Treaty was extremely general on the subject of what that should be, and the CAP was only slowly put in place, the crucial decisions being taken in 1963–64.

In those days, even the Community of Six was not self-sufficient in the main agricultural products and so the mechanisms of the CAP, largely invented by the French to ensure that French production gradually increased its share of the Community market, were not as economically undesirable as they are today. Simplifying a little, the system is based on guaranteed prices, with the Community buying-in products which farmers cannot sell on the market at those prices; on 'Community preference', that is to say, a system of import levies to ensure that agricultural produce imported from outside the Community cannot undercut Community products; on export 'restitutions', the jargon for subsidies to bridge the often large gap between Community and world prices and thus to help dispose of products surplus to Community requirements; and on common financing through the Community budget.

It is worth noting that there is no theoretical reason why such a system (except for export restitutions) should produce ever-growing surpluses, or even surpluses at all. If the guaranteed prices were set at levels which caused the farmers to produce the quantity of food which people in the Community want to eat (and need to store against a rainy day), plus whatever could be exported at world market prices, plus whatever the Council decides to give away in food aid, all would be fairly well, except probably for farmers' incomes.

One of the main reasons why all is not well is that German prices, particularly for cereals, which are the key product in the system, were far higher than French prices before the Community was founded and the German Government refused then, and has refused ever since, to bring them down to an economic level. The common prices were thus set too high at the beginning, and this mistake has been compounded since by two additional factors:

First – the Agricultural Council, which fixes the prices each year, naturally is extremely sensitive to the powerful farmers' lobby and, as we all know, farmers will tell you that they are virtually starving, even in the years when they make good profits;

Second – the differing rates of inflation and productivity in the member states led to a series of devaluations of the franc and the lira, and revaluations

35

of the mark and the florin; and the ways these exchange rate problems have been dealt with have resulted in still higher common prices.

The monetary problem has given rise to a great deal of confusion and acrimony. In the sixties, the French sought to deal with it by inventing a system of 'Monetary Compensatory Amounts', i.e. of border taxes and subsidies within the Community. Countries with appreciating currencies (always the Germans) were allowed, after an ordinary Deutschmark re-valuation, to maintain the same Deutschmark prices to their farmers through 'positive' MCAs, i.e. the Community imposed taxes at the German border on imports into Germany and provided subsidies at the border on German exports, thus creating a 'green' mark and, for example, guilder with a different parity from the real mark or guilder. For depreciating currencies, such as the franc and the lira, the opposite took place and negative MCAs were created, creating a green franc and lira diverging in the opposite direction. The trouble was that each year the pressure grew on the French and Italian government from their farmers to devalue the green franc or lira and thus provide a higher guaranteed price level in France or Italy to compensate for inflation. By convention, the Agriculture Ministers made little fuss about devaluing green currencies with negative MCAs.

Though the German consumer would have been benefited by revaluations of the green mark, these on the other hand only took place when the other member states brought great pressure to bear on Germany because successive German governments never wanted to alienate their farmers by lowering Deutschmark prices. As a result German production was stimulated more than it should have been, German exports of expensive products grew, and the French began to regret inventing MCA's because of the competitive advantage they were giving to Germany (and Holland).

The MCA system is not easy to understand. Those readers who are having trouble following the argument may take some comfort from the fact that incoming Foreign Secretaries always found it more of a headache than most Community subjects. Yet they had to grasp all the implications. In the days when the pound was very low, in the mid nineteen-seventies, the government had to consider from time to time whether to give the farmers a better price by devaluing the green pound. When the pound rose in the early nineteen-eighties and Britain switched to having positive MCAs, the farmers naturally wanted things left as they were, while the consumer lobby was in favour of revaluation. No modern Foreign Secretary can opt out of such decisions which have profound consequences for farmers as well as for the Community budget.

It is not necessary to go into the monetary question further here, because the French have now finally persuaded the Germans to commit themselves to doing away with 'positive' MCAs; in return for which they joined in getting the Council to agree that, in future, when currencies are realigned, the guaranteed price will move with the strongest currency. This undesirable solution means that, for example, as a result of the realignment of currencies of July 1985, when the Italians devalued by 6% and all the other members of the European Monetary System exchange rate mechanism revalued by 2% the Italians were in due course able to raise their prices by 8% by devaluing the green lira; or that as a result of the more general realignment of April 1986, the French will eventually be able to devalue the green franc by the full measure of their devaluation against the D-mark (or 5.8%) instead of their devaluation against the central rate of 2.8%, increasing prices in France accordingly.

Alas! – few of the governments seem to be able to resist their farmers' lobby. Every spring, the Commission makes relatively rigorous price proposals which the British frequently are almost alone in supporting. Every spring, most representatives of the member states in the Special Committee on Agriculture (which prepares the Council) say these are not generous enough and, for good measure, put in a number of bids for special treatment for some section of their farming community. The Agriculture Council then gradually puts together a package deal which gives all the member states a measure of satisfaction and in the end not only agree on a price level higher than the Commission proposes, but also distribute small but significant presents all round. 1986 was more rigorous than usual, but, alas, not rigorous enough!

The accession of Britain, Denmark and Ireland to the Community in 1973 brought in two net exporting countries – Denmark and Ireland, and one major net importer, Britain. The CAP suited Denmark and Ireland very well, but not the UK as a country. For one thing it was the main cause of the British budget problem, with which I shall deal later. But it suited the British farmers pretty well, and the bigger farmers extremely well. The UK percentage of self-sufficiency for the main products we produce has been rising rapidly ever since. During the first decade or so of our membership (1973–1984), Ministry of Agriculture statistics show our self-sufficiency ratio up from

74% to 90% for meat

41% to 77% for milk products

35% to 55% for sugar and

65% to 109% for cereals

It is the success of the farmers in Britain and elsewhere in increasing their productivity that is causing the Community's problems. Despite serious efforts by the Commission since 1981 and relative restraint by the Council since 1983, reform of the CAP is not even keeping up with the worsening of the situation. The financial consequences for the Community have become serious. The CAP is still taking 70% of a much larger budget. Far too late, action has begun to be taken to curb the surpluses. In 1984, with milk production at 120% or more of consumption, a quota system with a cutback of 4% or 5% was agreed; and in 1986 a further gradual cutback was agreed. But these quotas are unpopular and a bad solution in the long run; difficult and costly to administer fairly and, like all quota systems, economically inefficient. Quotas for cereals would be even more difficult to impose. Yet productivity is rising fast while markets may even be shrinking.

It is the difference between Community prices and world prices which determines the cost of CAP because the surpluses are mostly disposed of on world markets with the export subsidies set at a level which make them attractive to buyers. World prices for agricultural products have only been above Community prices in one year, 1974–75. Fortunately for the pro-Market cause, that was the year of the Referendum! World prices remain low today and it is difficult to see any reason why they should rise. Since most of them are denominated in dollars, every percentage point of decline in the dollar vis-à-vis the ECU is liable to increase the gap between world prices and Community prices and is estimated to cost the Community budget 100 million ECUs. This has been a major factor in the cost of the CAP since February 1985.

Among the Community's best customers for subsidized exports are the Russians who are delighted to buy butter at a fraction of the Community price. This has always outraged ordinary people in Britain who see no advantage whatever in using the taxpayer's money to enable the Soviet Government to sell butter to their people more cheaply than it is sold in British supermarkets – and still to make a profit on the transaction. It is the point to which people always return when the pros and cons of the Community are under discussion. Personally I share the view that these sales to Russia are politically and economically indefensible. But, except to some extent in Germany and Holland, they do not seem to arouse the same furious reaction in other Community countries.

As subsidized Community exports have grown, the other main agricultural exporters, led by the United States – though themselves far from innocent of subsidizing their agriculture – have become increasingly and self-righteously determined to do something about the CAP. They claim that European exports are making inroads into their markets in third countries. With American agriculture in deep trouble, it is going to be a superhuman task to keep US–

European relations in regard to agricultural trade on an even keel.

This is not the place to try to discuss fully the options for CAP reform. Good and simple alternative solutions have not appeared. Some member states, for example, advocate a tax on imported oils and fats. But this would be contrary to the Community's international commitments and thus certain to exacerbate the Community's strained relations with the USA, as well as to raise prices to consumers. To drop the prices to a market-clearing level would require a very large reduction and would have political and social effects on the farmers which the governments cannot accept. To follow that course and to make up the difference to the farmers by social subsidies would be politically unattractive because the farmerss like to think that they are getting their money from 'the Market', would be difficult to administer and might cost even more than the CAP in its present form. To convert the butter into biodegradable plastic or the wine into car fuel is technically possible but uneconomic. To create more national parks would take some land out of production, but productivity increases would soon nullify the effect. To put a high tax on fertilizers would perhaps reduce yields, but would put up the price of food and make Europe even less competitive on world markets. To pay the farmers not to produce (for example, to plant trees) might cost less (as well as being good for the environment provided there was a mixture of hard and soft woods). But how to do it in the long run? There are no good, cheap answers to the agricultural problems.

The Finance Ministers have done their best to impose discipline. In 1985, they agreed after long and painful negotiations on a financial guideline, formally incorporated in the Ecofin Council's conclusions on budget and discipline, under which the cost of the CAP should in future grow less rapidly than the Community's revenue base. But the late 1985/early 1986 fall of the dollar against the ECU and the cost of disposing of existing surpluses has already made it impossible to keep within the guideline, without farmers all over the Community even having to come out onto the roads in their tractors, overturning truckloads of surplus products in inconvenient places.

There is no single solution and, in any case, even now, not enough support to put through root-and-branch reform in one major push. But one thing is certain – unless there is more radical action in the immediate future, the CAP is at serious risk of collapse for lack of funds and the Community will suffer from the quarrels that this would cause. That is not to say that it would be against the long-term interests of the Community as a whole if the CAP came gradually to place a greater financial burden on those governments whose countries benefit most from it. Then all Agricultural Ministers would then have to be more careful about supporting expensive price-fixing deals each year.

Some combination of the remedies just briefly canvassed will in the end have to be applied. In my own view, to be effective, these should include *all* the following:

(1) Assuming a continuing German veto on price cuts, a price freeze lasting several years in terms of the strongest currency (Deutschmarks, no doubt), on all products in surplus;

(2) Some *extra* penalty on cereal production, whether a tax on fertilizers or a 'co-responsibility' levy (see below) or quotas;

(3) Gradual reduction in milk and sugar quotas, new olive oil quotas, more stringent control of wine production;

(4) Some support on social grounds for small and disadvantaged farmers, perhaps with the cost shared between the Community budget at, say 25% and the national budgets at 75%. It would be essential to share the costs in this way. If the Community budget bore the whole cost, a qualified majority in the Agriculture Council would probably push the cost up to unbearable levels. If national budgets bore the whole cost, the Community would have no say in the level of subsidies and unfair competition would be certain to result. A 25:75 ratio would give both the Community and national Finance Ministers the right degree of leverage.

(5) An agreement with the United States and other major producers to avoid a price-cutting/export-subsidy war, but involving on the Community side a commitment to a gradual lowering of export subsidies, e.g. a 10% decline in volume of money spent each year.

(6) Subsidies for planting trees, particularly hardwood, on ground previously farmed and the creation of new national parks on farmland.

In its late-April decisions on the 1986 price-fixing the Agriculture Council went quite some way towards this programme (written in January 1986) – somewhat to my surprise! But the EMS realignment which had first taken place made it possible for the Council to accept a price freeze and yet to give a price increase to most member states, though not of course to Germany which again revalued (the mark and the guilder remained the strongest currencies).

It is not always easy for outsiders to see what is happening. For example, the Commission proposed a 'co-responsibility' levy on cereals, i.e. a tax to help pay for disposal. Combined with a price freeze, such a levy is, of course, a rigorous measure. It is another way of reducing the price to producers. But if it is combined with a price rise, it is simply a concealed way of increasing the money available to the CAP. In the past when co-responsibility levies were imposed on milk, they were combined with price rises. As the discussions in the 1985 price-fixing showed, there are several other ways in which a nominal price freeze can be transformed into a real price increase. This year, however, the Agriculture Council accepted a co-responsibility levy of 3% on cereals without putting up the basic price. Alas, this new rigour has come too late to stop the CAP from pushing the budget up against its new ceiling. Only a 'miracle' like several disastrous world harvests can save the CAP from a serious financing crisis!

3

The Internal Market, Industry, Technology and Research

HERE WE COME to the central question for the late 1980s. Can the Community with reasonable speed turn Western Europe as a whole (for the EFTA countries will follow the Community) into a single great market almost like the United States market, without significant barriers to doing business in goods or services or to capital movements? And will this increase European competitivity and dynamism and thus provide jobs, making Europe richer and socially and politically more stable?

The answer to both questions must be Yes. A single great market would be certain to boost trade and increased production regularly goes with increased trade. The cost to producers of the remaining barriers to free trade in goods and services such as delays at frontiers (several billion pounds a year) and wasting time with bureaucratic controls is enormous. A young Belgian businessman on the export sales side of his firm recently told me that he had to allow three or four times as long for Customs and other government controls as he did for making a sale. The costs to consumers are high too. Think only of the astronomical difference it would have made to car buyers in the UK over the past fifteen years if they had been able to buy cars at Belgian prices.

But the most important factor would be that European companies competing in a Europe-wide market, with the possible economies of scale which would be involved, ought to become more efficient. In discussing the problems of European industry, we must always keep in the forefront of our minds the paramount need for European companies to be able to compete successfully in world markets. Protectionism leads to inefficiency, whether it is on a national or a European basis. The single great market will help to improve competitivity, but it must remain part of the open world trading system under the GATT, and will not therefore absolve European companies from the need to be sufficiently efficient to compete successfully with the Americans, Japanese and newly industrialising countries.

Whether the single great market can be more or less completed by 1992 (as agreed by Heads of Government in Luxembourg in December 1985) is largely a matter of will and effort. To read the Commission's White Paper of June 1985, an arduous task in itself, is to realise how much remains to be done. Here is a sample of priority tasks:

Frontier clearance

–   Simplification of documentation, especially putting the Single Administrative Document (now accepted in the Council) into operation to replace the 15–20 documents still required.
–   Cost-effective co-ordination of customs computerisation throughout the Community, to facilitate more rapid clearance of goods and to open the possibility of a 'single declarant', thus avoiding unnecessary duplication of information at export and import.
–   Abolition of duty on fuel in tanks at borders.

Standards for industrial products

–   Rapid implementation of the new initiative for the mutual recognition of standards rather than detailed harmonisation.
–   Speedy establishment of testing and certification systems, to ensure the free flow of products meeting standards acceptable under the initiative.

Liberalisation of financial services

–   Early adoption of the non-life insurance services directive to allow insurers to write business freely throughout the Community.
–   Abolition of exchange controls.
–   Liberalisation of the securities market, equities, gilts and investment management and advice, and mutual access to Stock Exchange listings and co-operation between exchanges.
–   Liberalisation of Public Purchasing. A vital step in the field of telecommunications and other high technology industries.

Liberalisation of Transport

–   Inland transport: liberalisation of international road haulage, especially the abolition of the quotas for lorries.
–   Air transport: much greater competition through significant liberalisation of the present heavily regulated system (liberalisation of market access;

relaxation of strict fifty-fifty sharing of capacity on routes; freedom for airlines to set fares on the basis of their commercial judgement).

– Sea transport: the adoption of rules which would set a timetable for the elimination of all restrictions on the freedom to provide shipping services to, from, between, and within member states.

State Aids

– A more rigorous appoach is required than in the past, in order to prevent the single market being undermined by rival state aids.

This is only a short list of high priorities. The Commission claims that it is a serious mistake for any member government genuinely keen on completing the internal market, as the British are, to pick and choose items among the three hundred in their White Paper. This, they argue, will lead to others doing the same, with different priorities, after which the Council will become blocked for lack of agreement on where to start. Alas, this scenario is not incredible. But the thesis that the Commission White Paper must be, or has been (at the European Council at Milan in June 1985,) accepted as a whole *is* incredible. First, the Milan Council did lay down some priority areas, not so very different from those set out above. Second, whatever happens, the White Paper will not be implemented lock, stock and barrel.

The Commission included 'approximation' (i.e. bringing within, say, 5% of each other) of national VAT and excise taxes in their 1992 programme. There are a majority of member governments who do not want to do this in a hurry. Some are concerned about losing flexibility for their own government financing if they have to 'approximate'. Others have relatively high or low VAT or excise taxes and do not want to change them. Yet others, such as the UK, have always had VAT zero rates on quite a wide range of goods or services and would find it politically difficult to charge VAT on these at any percentage. That is why, at the Milan Council, it was agreed that this subject should be taken out of the internal market package and studied by the ECOFIN (Finance Ministers') Council.

My own belief is that taxation is a field in which the market itself should be allowed to produce solutions. If there is completely free trade of goods and services, member governments with high VAT or excise rates will probably find that they are losing sales to cross-border buying. The necessary degree of approximation will not be slow to follow. And the degree to which different rates can be lived with can only be established by experience, as it has been in the United States with the different sales taxes in different states.

The Commission's White Paper has run into trouble for another reason – and one which could have been avoided. The Delors Commission, early in its life, adopted the attractive goal of a Europe without frontiers. That is what Ernest Bevin said we should aim for in 1946. It is what Europe always had until the last century or so of its history. Most people would vote for it as a long-term aim. But it is not the same thing as the single great market. The Commission's mistake was to equate the two things.

You can have free movement of goods and services without abolishing frontiers. You cannot abolish frontiers without doing many things which you do not need to do in order to complete the internal market. Immigration controls will be required on the Community's internal frontiers until all member states have an effective common policy on immigration from outside (which will not be by 1992). Without internal frontiers, the task of catching terrorists and drug traffickers would be made harder. Those countries which do not have identity cards would probably have to introduce them. The British will continue to insist that frontier controls are essential to keep out rabid dogs. None of these difficulties can be removed at a wave of the wand and so in my view the Commission would have done better to stick to the definition of the internal market which is implicit in the relevant chapters of the Treaty of Rome, freedom to trade in goods, to provide services, to move capital, and to take jobs in other countries. It is doubtful whether this controversy will have been permanently stilled by the adoption of the following sentence by the European Council in Luxembourg in December 1985: 'The internal market shall comprise an area without internal frontiers in which the free movement of goods, persons, services and capital is ensured in accordance with the provisions of the Treaty'. Even though there is an agreed Council Declaration which supports a restrictive interpretation, the words themselves come close to adopting both sides of a contradiction. However, the decision will allow work to go forward and it is hard to see how the issue could come before the European Court until after 1992.

To mention these reservations about the White Paper is not to play down its crucial importance. The unity of the market is one of the great issues of the late 1980s and the benefits of achieving it by 1992 will be large, politically as well as economically.

EUROPEAN HIGH TECHNOLOGY INDUSTRY

Europe is doing relatively badly in the so-called 'sunrise industries', such as information technology, and completing the internal market can only be a part of the solution. Nor is the main obstacle to success any lack of inventions or deficiencies in research (though a pooling of research efforts could improve the cost/benefit ratio for the money spent). What needs to be done is to facilitate the creation of enterprises capable of taking advantage of a Europe-wide market and thus succeeding in the competition for world market share. In information technology and other high technology industries, which provide an increasing percentage of the industrialised world's production each year, a company must achieve a reasonable percentage (say at least 5%) of the world market in order to succeed. It is no longer enough to do well in the home market of a medium-sized country such as Britain, France or Germany. European high technology industry will not be made to flourish by the creation of successful small and medium-sized enterprises, however desirable that may be. The investments required to gain 5% of the world market and climb upwards from there are large.

In 1975, the European balance of trade in information technology was still positive, but since the beginning of the 1980s there has been a deficit of the order of US $6 billion per year. Between 1978 and 1984, the European share of the European information technology industry fell from 44.6% to 39.4%. In 1978, the ten top-ranking producers of semiconductors worldwide included two European companies. In 1984, only one European country is left and this one has fallen back from fourth to seventh place.

European industry in many sectors, particularly those dominated by public purchasing, is still showing a 'national champion' attitude. For example, European countries have developed ten different digital switching systems at an estimated cost of US $10 billion, while US expenditure by three companies has been US $3 billion and Japanese expenditure by two companies US $1.5 billion. There is certainly not a market for ten different European products, possibly only for one or two, and it is not the European companies who are winning the lion's share of the contracts. If European companies do not get together, they will go to the wall.

Responsible people have been known to argue that it does not much matter whether European consumers are provided for by European industry or by American or Japanese multinationals, particularly those with a manufacturing capability in Europe. This form of allegedly benign indifference is dangerous. The aim of American or Japanese multinationals is to increase the profits of the parent company based in the US or Japan and to transmit the profits to the parent company. They naturally do the major part of their research at home, financed out of these profits. If necessary for a time, in order to conquer the European market, the parent company may well decide to invest in a plant in Europe, even to do some of its research in Europe. But once the European

46

competition is knocked out, there will be very little reason for the parent company to invest further in Europe rather than at home or perhaps in some third country whose market remains to be conquered. And most of the benefits of the profits of the parent company will continue to flow to its own economy. Let no one misunderstand what I am saying. I am not arguing against American or Japanese investment in Europe, only that it is undesirable for them to knock out or take over all the main European companies in their field.

I do not propose to debate the Westland affair. I was out of government by the time the argument broke out and probably not in possession of all the facts. But I was on the inside of the very similar but less dramatic argument about British Aerospace and Airbus during the Callaghan Government's last two years. British Aerospace was faced with the choice between a superficially attractive offer from Boeing to co-operate on building their 757 aircraft and getting fully into Airbus with a 20% share of the enterprise. British Airways, very pro-Boeing, and Rolls Royce, unfortunately not yet convinced that it would pay them to produce an engine for Airbus and hoping to get into a leading position to provide an engine for the 757, argued for the Boeing option. British Aerospace, farsightedly in my view, argued that this would make them almost totally dependent on Boeing in the civil aircraft field. Even if co-operation on the 757 turned out to be more than sub-contracting, which was far from proven, they would have no bargaining power for the future and therefore no means of securing even as favourable terms as for the 757 in relation to a successor aircraft. They would loose out in the vital fields of research and aircraft design. As in all such arguments, people become heated. The Boeing camp denigrated Airbus vigorously, and in the light of hindsight wrongly. British Aerospace argued that partnership in Airbus was the better option for assuring their long-term future in major civil aircraft.

The Government was inevitably drawn into the argument. To rejoin Airbus it was necessary not only for British Aerospace to reach agreement with the French and German companies but also for the Government to do so with their governments. In the end this was achieved, not without warm arguments within Government, and British Aerospace was saved from becoming dependent on Boeing. The European option was, of course, not without risk. But British Aerospace were surely right in the light of hindsight to go for it, even if Airbus as a whole is taking a long time to bring in profits.

In my view, Europe cannot afford to let United States and Japanese multinationals dominate these high technology markets. It is not only the fact that the profits of multinationals go to the home country and any investment in Europe is pretty mobile and not necessarily long-term. There are other risks.

The Boeings and IBMs of this world cannot behave in too overtly a monopolist or oligopolist way now, as they work to dominate the market still more than at present. But if there were no prospect of viable European competitors, they would be bound to be tempted to do so or at least to form some sophisticated modern version of a cartel with the Japanese to keep up prices and keep European competitors from springing up to gnaw away at this position at the edges. Would Boeing prices now be as low as they are if Airbus was not there to provide the necessary competition? To allow American or Japanese multi-nationals to get into a monopoly or oligopoly position would be bad for the ordinary consumer, but also dangerous for the health of the rest of European industry which will be increasingly dependent on high technology products in such fields as information technology and robotics.

Relations with the United States in these fields are a delicate matter. Even marginal discrimination in favour of genuinely European companies, i.e. companies with their headquarters in Europe and with European countries as the principal beneficiaries from the profits, could add to the trade difficulties between the Community and the United States. But we must not forget that the Americans discriminate vigorously in favour of American companies. The Buy American Act remains in force, but this is not the main factor. The Pentagon and NASA have very different ways of pushing the contracts to the American firms of their choice. Local and state governments can also discriminate in favour of American companies. During the last five years, there has been a steady tightening by the United States government as far as the transfer of technology from the United States to Europe is concerned. It is claimed that this is in order to stop it going to the Soviet Union, but most observers feel that commercial considerations *vis-à-vis* especially Japan but also Europe play a part in American motives. Finally, the American defence procurement and space programmes and now SDI are not only subsidising Europe's American competitors but also tempting away management and scientific talent from Europe to America with vast financial rewards.

It is because IBM and other American and Japanese companies have with great care been building up a position in the European Community over the years (and in the process representing themselves as European companies), that the completion of the internal market can only be part of the answer to the problem of how to help genuinely European companies to survive into the 1990s and the next century. More than one European industrialist has said to me in private that they fear that it will be the American and Japanese multinationals who profit more than anyone else if they are allowed to draw all the advantages that the opening up of public purchasing and other internal market measures will provide without any reciprocity for European firms in the American and Japanese markets.

It is twenty years ago since Servan-Schreiber wrote *Le Défi Américain* and yet so little has been done to remedy a steadily worsening situation. Why is this? It is partly national public purchasing, which has scarcely been dented by twenty eight years of the Common Market. It is partly nationalism in government subsidies and industry conspiring with government to secure subsidies to help national champions to survive in isolation. There are also objective difficulties in the way of building European companies which through co-operation, joint ventures or merger become of a size and strength capable of seizing 5% of the world market.

Co-operation between companies at the pure research end of the spectrum is possible and was beginning in the information technology field in the 1970s. But as soon as you get nearer to the product or network systems required in order to gain market share, each company becomes extremely reluctant to share its ideas with others whom it regards as its competitors.

Moreover, and very important, the national governments and the European Community have not taken the necessary steps to provide the right climate for co-operation. The national governments have competed with each other to subsidise Japanese or American inward investment in a fashion best calculated to make these formidably predatory competitors still more successful in putting Europeans out of business. The Commission, on occasion, and some of the national monopoly bodies, especially the German Kartelamt, have interpreted the competition and national aids rules in so rigid a way as to make European co-operation more difficult. Can this really be sensible when competition from outside the Community, from Japan and America, is always going to be quite sufficient to keep European industry fighting to improve productivity and competitiveness?

There has been no incentive to European co-operation. Indeed, for example, the British Business Expansion Scheme is so drafted that it does not apply to co-operative ventures with non-British companies. The European Community needs, in parallel with its effort to complete the internal market, to make a concentrated attack on all these problems.

But let us be clear that there are some things which, while superficially attractive from the point of view of European companies, the Community would be most unwise to do. First, it should be beware of the argument that tariff protection should be afforded to 'infant' European industries trying to establish themselves in high technology fields. We are talking about gaining an adequate share of the global market. To try to keep the Americans and

Japanese out of the European market might well fail and would certainly not help to compete with them elsewhere. Second, the governments and the Commission must neither attempt to do industry's job for it by trying themselves to pick the winners, nor increase the bureaucratic and regulatory burden on industry in the name of acting to promote co-operation between European companies. Third, whatever is done must be consistent with the Community's obligations in GATT and elsewhere; and must be fully discussed with the Community's trading partners. We will not make things better by contributing to a trade war breaking out. But there is much that could be done within these parameters.

The Americans would be badly placed, for example, to complain if the Community took a leaf out of their book and explained to them that international arrangements must be based on reciprocity. If Buy American and other US discrimination in favour of their own companies are not to be scrapped, they must be matched in Europe. If different rules are applied to American companies as far as the transfer of technology is concerned, the Americans must not complain if we adopt measures to promote co-operation between genuinely European companies, i.e. companies with their head-quarters in Europe and with the bulk of their profits flowing into European countries. (Despite IBM's great efforts to present itself as a European company, the US Government knows that it is an American company and makes IBM in Europe comply with its rules on the transfer of technology.) It would be nonsense to take action to help European companies to co-operate with each other and compete with American multinationals and then to extend all the benefits to the European subsidiaries of those same multinationals because they do some of their work in Europe.

Mrs Thatcher's proposal before the Milan European Council in June 1985 for a 'Euro-type Warrant' was an important contribution to the debate. Under this proposal two or more genuinely European companies co-operating together to produce a new high technology product would be able to apply for a warrant (something like, but not quite like, a patent) which would guarantee the holder the most-favoured treatment available in all member states as far as investment incentives and public purchasing are concerned.

The European Commission is pondering this subject deeply. President Delors was attracted by the Euro-type Warrant idea and determined that the Commission shall make a major effort to create the conditions in which European high technology industry can co-operate to survive. Some people in the Commission are tempted to think either that Community research is the answer or that renewed work on a European company statute should be the main focus. As for research, it is important, but only marginally important in this connection. European companies are not losing out for lack of invention. As for the European company it is true that there are legal and fiscal obstacles to setting up a company which can operate Europe-wide, as Rob Wilmott has found in connection with his venture ES^2, a genuinely European company incorporated in Luxembourg, designed to take a major share of the market for custom chips. It is also true that the forms of co-operation adopted in the aircraft industry, both civil and military (Airbus and Tornado), are less than ideal from the point of view of efficiency. But in my view much more urgent action is required than to resume intensive work on the European Company Statute which would certainly take many years. Simpler methods need to be found to make it easier to form enterprises like ES^2.

The moment is ripe to move. People's minds, both in government and industry, have changed a great deal in the last year or two and there is now wide recognition that Europe risks being left without an effective high technology industry in the next century if urgent action is not taken. We need a package of decisions in the Council – to introduce something like the Euro-type Warrant with a satisfactory definition of a genuinely European company; to adapt the national and Community rules of competition, both as regards mergers and state aids, to ensure that they do not hinder joint action in Europe where outside competition is available; to promote a self-denying ordinance in all member countries against bribing high technology companies from outside to invest in Europe to the detriment of indigenous companies (the Japanese and Americans do not do it for Europeans investing in their countries and will invest in Europe even if they are not bribed); to counter the Buy American Act either by matching it with, for example, a Buy European Act or, better still, negotiating it away by threatening to match it; to take a common position towards the US Government in order to get less damaging rules on the transfer of technology to European companies; finally, co-ordinating and adapting national schemes for promoting innovation and providing incentives to new enterprises so that they push in the direction of European co-operation and not against it.

The reader may wonder why I have not yet mentioned Eureka, which is a forum for promoting European co-operation, bringing together both Community and non-Community West European countries. In my view, this 1985 initiative by France was an imaginative one though it is still unclear in mid-1986 exactly what role it may have. It focused attention on the problem at the right psychological moment. It has given a boost to discussion of solutions such as the Euro-type Warrant. It may result in governments nudging European companies into some co-operation in which they would not have otherwise engaged. But the actual measures which can be taken to create the right climate for co-operative enterprises, such as those just described, need to be taken in the European Community if they are to be transformed into law throughout the Community in the time-scale required.

Even though co-operation in research is only a small part of the answer to the problems of European high technology industry, it is important to organise it properly. There are strong reasons for thinking that much government-financed research in the Community would be more cost-effective if pooled and done by the Community. Both governments and the Community spend vast sums on research, the Council having already approved expenditure of over 1,000 million ECUs a year for the next five years and the Commission proposing still further large increases. A check list of the programmes (as agreed at end-1985) and their estimated cost is in an Appendix to this chapter.

In a number of fields, national governments are spending money on the same sort of basic research in two, three or even more countries. But there are many obstacles to any rapid move towards pooling. Firstly, chief Scientists in government departments throughout the Community will explain to you with conviction and detailed arguments which are difficult to refute why their programmes are of special value and must be maintained. It is human nature that they should be so convinced. What each man does himself seems the more significant because he does it.

Secondly, Community research did not win widespread praise in its first decade or so. The biggest project at the Joint Research Centre, engagingly named Super-Sara but glaringly not cost-effective, had to be scrapped. With the new programmes, Esprit, Brite, and Race (see Appendix) the reputation of Community research is improving. The Chief Scientific Advisor to a major continental company told me in 1985 that he had come round to the view that the current rating for Community research should be after company but before government research in his country. All the same, it will need time and sustained good performance before government scientists start to choose European projects rather than their own if they have to choose between them.

Thirdly – and this is the crucial difficulty – , it is objectively difficult to agree on priorities and phasing. Existing national programmes do not cover exactly the same ground or end at the same time. So the timing of any move to joint research is always tricky.

There are, however, some projects which have to be done by the Community if they are to be done at all. JET (at Culham, near Oxford), which is a major and very expensive project looking into the possibility of controlling fusion as a source of clean energy in the next century, is a perfect example. No European government would have done on its own. But there are not many necessary projects on this scale; even JET itself is not without its critics.

To get an idea of the scope of the Community Research and Development, the Summary in the appendix may prove useful. Davignon's idea of promoting research co-operation in the information technology field (Esprit) by bringing together the main companies at a Round Table and planning with them a programme made up of a large number of relatively small research projects, seems a good model. Esprit is financed 50/50 by the Community and the companies (1500 million ECUs over five years) and undertaken under contract by groups including companies, research institutes and universities. It has certainly produced a lot of research co-operation, even if some participants say that setting this up has taken too much of the scarcest resource, researchers' time.

It is far from clear, however, how much, if at all, a programme like Esprit will help to push European companies to co-operate at the production/sales end of the spectrum. Esprit is at the pure research end and Davignon's original idea, now to be followed up by the Commission if the governments agree, was to move Esprit II nearer to the marketplace. In my view a larger Esprit II on these lines deserves support.

The picture of Community research so far is thus patchy, with bright and dark areas. The senior officials in the Commission now running Community programmes – Carpentier, especially, Fasella and Dinkespiler – are dedicated and impressive. But it will not be easy for the Commission to persuade the net contributor countries – Britain, France and Germany – to add huge sums to the existing five-year research programme when funds are short. (The Commission are talking of doubling the existing level to 2,000 million ECUs a year.) In my view, the tests for any proposal for a project or programme must continue to be: first, of course, whether there is a *prima facie* case that the research needs to be done; second, whether there are reasons for thinking that it will be done more cost-effectively in common. The second factor is crucial and difficult to judge. It has to include the benefits of not doing the same thing in two, three or four European countries. The facts are not always easy to establish. Government scientists on whom Ministers have no choice but to rely for advice are often reluctant to turn the thumbs-down on their own national projects in favour of common action. This subject is therefore likely to remain controversial during the next year or two.

If the European industry is only doing moderately well in the industries of the future, it has even more severe problems in some of the old industries. Steel is the prime example and it so happens that the Commission, having taken over the powers of the High Authority of the Coal and Steel Community, is in a position to take more direct action in regard to steel than in regard to other products. The ECSC Treaty of 1951 was considerably more 'supra-national' than the EEC Treaty (of Rome) of 1957.

In the late 1970s, it became evident that the steel market in the Community and indeed the industrialised world as a whole, was in crisis. Demand was stagnant or in decline; new capacity was coming onstream in developing countries; excess capacity in the Community was being maintained as a result of subsidies; and prices were being forced down to grossly uneconomic levels. The Commission estimated that there was around 50 million tonnes of excess Community capacity in hot rolled steel-making, or nearly one third of the total EEC capacity. Attempts to tackle these problems through voluntary means (notably output quotas agreed at industry level and exhortations to re-structure) failed. In the end, after long discussion and on a proposal by Davignon, a state of 'manifest crisis' in the sense of Article 58 of the ECSC Treaty was declared in October 1980. Once the Council had given its assent, the way was open to lay down production quotas, control prices and limit imports. Under the Davignon plan there were two main elements:

- short term market measures, in particular output quotas under Article 58 ECSC, later backed up by mandatory minimum prices for certain products and strict monitoring of cross-border intra-Community steel trade movements; and voluntary restraint arrangements limiting third country imports; all this intended to restore stability and provide a breathing space for restructuring;
- strict rules on the provision of state aids to the steel industry, under which all such aids had to be phased out by the end of 1985, and any granted meanwhile linked to a restructuring plan intended to restore the company concerned to viability, i.e. reductions in steel capacity.

As a result of these measures, the market has gradually stabilised and the worst forms of cut-throat competition have been avoided. By the end of 1985, 30 to 35 million tonnes of EEC steel-making capacity will have been elimin-ated, compared with 1980 levels. Prices have at last moved back closer to levels at which efficient companies can operate viably, and a number of European steel-makers are once more operating profitably. The Davignon plan not only encouraged these developments, but allowed them to happen in an orderly way, resisting the pressures (often evident in member states, particularly Germany) to 'compartmentalise' the Common Market, i.e. to keep out steel from other Community countries.

The story is not, however, over. A number of companies will have the greatest difficulty in meeting the current policy deadline for phasing out state aids next year; and in their document 'General Objectives Steel 1990', the Commission estimated that excess capacity of 20-25 million tonnes persists in the Community. Getting rid of this will be even more difficult to achieve than the first 30-35 million tonnes.

Of course, it would have been infinitely preferable not to have had a crisis and not therefore to have had to install a crisis régime. But the way it was managed, including the extremely difficult negotiations about voluntary restraints on Community exports to the United States, whose industry was also in crisis, does the Commission great credit. The European steel industry was carried along by a mixture of carrot and stick. Major inequities were avoided. The aim of returning to the free market was kept constantly in the foreground. The European steel industry was fortunate to have Davignon as its Commissioner during the five years of most serious crisis.

After all the debate of the last five years it is hardly necessary to stress the importance of government in general not trying to do the job of market forces. If European industry starts to regain market share, especially in high technology fields, it will be primarily because of their own efforts and enterprise. But I believe that the examples briefly examined in this chapter do demonstrate that there is also an important role for the European Community. If it can, by adopting measures which improve the climate for effective European co-operation to meet the American and Japanese challenge, add 10–15% at the margin to European industry's chances, that could make quite a lot of difference to the outcome.

END 1985 CHECK LIST OF *MAIN* R & D PROGRAMMES

ENERGY

	Duration	Funding Million ECU
FUSION Supports JET (8% contribution) and national fusion R & D.	1985–89	690
RADIATION PROTECTION Safety work on radiation	1985–89	58
RADIOACTIVE WASTE Waste management studies and construction of pilot underground facilities	1985–89	62
NON-NUCLEAR ENERGY Solar, wind and geothermal energy. Energy from biomass. Energy conservation. Utilisation of solid fueld. Production and utilisation of new energy vectors. Optimisation of hydrocarbon production and use. Energy systems analysis and modelling.	1985–88	175
DECOMMISSIONING OF NUCLEAR INSTALLATIONS Common R & D approach towards decommissioning, including new techniques.	1984–88	12

INDUSTRY	Duration	Funding Million ECU

ESPRIT
Five main areas (i) advanced microelectronics capability, (ii) software technologies, (iii) advanced information processing, (iv) office systems, (v) computer integrated manufacture. — 1984–88 — 750

DATA PROCESSING
In two parts both extended during 1984. Supports standardisation activities for the present. Also assisted work on standards for public procurement, distributed data bases, software languages. — 1979–86 — 51

MICROELECTRONICS TECHNOLOGY
Now being overtaken by Esprit. — 1982–85 — 40

★BRITE
(Basic technological research and application of new technologies) New technologies for old industries e.g. lasers, joining techniques, use of new materials e.g. polymers. Sub-programme on new production technologies for the textile industry. — 1985–88 — 125

COMMUNITY BUREAU OF REFERENCE
Reference materials and applied metrology. — 1983–87 — 25

RACE
Research and Development in Advanced Communications Technologies for Europe.
Work on reference model for broadband communication network and exploratory studies on R & D technology needed.

1985–86   20

STEEL
Production, processing, steel properties and utilisation.

Indefinite   17 p.a.

BIOTECHNOLOGY
Basic biotechnological R & D, support banks and co-ordination of biotechnological activities.

1985–89   55

RAW MATERIALS
(i) Existing
metals and minerals, wood as a renewable raw material, recycling of non-ferrous metals and materials substitution and technology.

1982–85   54

(ii) Proposed
As above plus emphasis on new advanced materials (EURAM)

1986–89   110

OTHER

ENVIRONMENT
(i) Existing
Environmental pollution, conservation and climatology. R & D to support city directives.

1981–85   47

(ii) Proposed
As above plus major technological hazards, i.e. response to Bhopal/Seveso

1986–90   105

SCIENCE & TECHNOLOGY FOR DEVELOPMENT

R & D on tropical agriculture and medicine, health and nutrition for developing countries.

1983–86   40

AGRICULTURE

Utilisation and conservation of agricultural resources, structural aspects and improvement of animal and plant productivity.

1984–88   30

FAST

Programme on *F*orecasting and *A*ssessment in *S*cience and *T*echnology. Think tank type work analysing implications of scientific and technological changes.

1983–87   8.5

STIMULATION

Horizontal activity to aid mobility of researchers, twinning of laboratories and strengthening of communication and exchanges of information between labs.

1985–88   60

JOINT RESEARCH CENTRE

Main areas are:

1984–87   700
(+ updating
for staff
costs)

1. Industrial technologies
    Nuclear measurements and reference materials.
    High temperature materials.

92

2. Fusion technology and safety
    (including tritium laboratory)

59

3. Fission   352
   Reactor safety
   Radioactive waste
   Safeguarding fissile materials
   Nuclear fuels and actinides research.

4. Non-nuclear energy   39
   Solar energy
   Management of energy in dwellings.

5. Environment   99
   Environmental protection
   Remote sensing
   Industrial hazards

6. Operation of High Flux Reactor   59
                                                             (including
                                                             FRG and
                                                             Netherland
                                                          contributions)

[Note: R & D programmes are generally supported by all Member States with obvious preference of nuclear Member States for nuclear programmes. Participation varies according to scientific/industrial capability]

* Due for review summer 1986

4

Fisheries, The Environment, Rules of Competition and State Aids, Economic and Monetary Policy

THIS CHAPTER TREATS four important but disparate subjects which illustrate the diversity of the Community agenda: fisheries, where, without the specific authority of the Treaty, there is now a common policy which is as important for fishermen as the CAP is for the farmers; the environment, where, without any specific base in the Treaty (prior to ratification of the Treaty amendments agreed in Luxembourg in December 1985), there is an increasing number of agreed common rules; state aids and the rules of competition, where the Commission has important direct powers under the Treaty; and economic and monetary policy, where, in some respects, the Treaty is still not being observed and where one of the most important activities, the European Monetary System (EMS) has up to now been done outside it.

What these disparate subjects have in common, like most other subjects on the Community agenda (see end of this chapter), is that there are things which need to be done by European countries acting together. Of course, it would be theoretically possible to solve some of the problems in these areas by *ad hoc* intergovernmental agreements between sovereign countries instead of through the Community, but this would certainly be slower and probably less effective, for lack of common legislation. Those who complain, not always without justification, that the Community's decision-making processes are too slow should bear in mind that almost everything in this world is relative. Compared with the international work on the law of the sea, the unusually long-draw-out and painful negotiations on the Common fisheries policy were rather fast.

FISHERIES

The subject of fisheries does get a mention in the Treaty. Article 38 says that the Common Market shall extend to agriculture and trade in agricultural products and among the latter includes the products of fisheries. But it does not say that there shall be a Common Fisheries Policy as it does for the CAP.

The French, nevertheless, insisted in 1971, with British, Danish and Norwegian prospective membership and their importance as fishing nations in mind, that there must be a common fisheries policy established before the first enlargement. The other member states went along with this at a relatively late stage in the entry negotiations. This caused the UK and Denmark considerable difficulties at the time, but they swallowed the pill. Norway's referendum was however certainly adversely affected.

This policy, broadly speaking, provided for free access to all Community waters after a ten-year transitional period. The scope of this provision was vastly extended when the general move to 200-mile fishery limits took place in 1975–76. However, in the light of this extension, even the French were ready to accept that there could not be completely free access and that therefore a new common fisheries régime was required.

It was an exceptionally difficult subject, arousing strong emotions in maritime peoples. Fishermen are resistant to government control, determined to defend their historic rights to fish where they have always fished, and prone to feuds with fishermen from other countries. The British, especially the Scots, with the very considerable new areas of sea in which they would have exclusive rights if it were not for the common fisheries policy, found themselves in the front line. Ireland, Denmark, Germany, Holland, Belgium, and France all also have important fishing industries and constituencies in which fishermen's votes are of crucial importance. But the UK, contributing 60% of Community waters, found itself in the most difficult position.

A long and difficult negotiation began in 1976. Mr Crosland had just become Foreign Secretary and, coming from a fishing constituency, was acutely aware of the importance and delicacy of the problem. He set out to try to find a solution but, sadly in any case and most unfortunately from the fisheries point of view, he died before he could get very far. During the remainder of the life of the Labour Government no progress was made.

When the Conservative Government came to power, they set out on a prudent and tough negotiation in order to try to get a settlement. It took three years and the final compromise was detailed and complicated. In brief, Community waters were divided up into different zones. Total Allowable Catches (TACs) and quotas were fixed for each important species for each zone. Quotas were allocated to member states in percentages of the TACs, the quantities but not the percentages being reviewed each year. In addition, fairly rigorous direct conservation measures were agreed, such as the temporary ban on herring fishing (not always observed by all fishermen, least of all by the

Dutch, who have a passion for young herring) and rules about the sizes of nets and about the quantity of other species that can be caught with the main target fish (bye catches). At the beginning of 1985, a small Inspectorate was created, the first Community Police Force, and is apparently doing good work.

Conservation is at the heart of the CAP and is something which is far better done on a Community than a national basis. Shoals of fish are not prone to respect national fishery limits any more than fishermen. But at least some control can be exercised over the fishermen while the fish will continue to go their own way.

The TACs are fixed for each species in the light of scientific advice about what the stocks in the sea will bear. The rules about net-sizes and bye-catches are designed to prevent fishing for one species wiping out others. The herring ban, even if not completely observed, has resulted in the stock being rebuilt to the point where fishing can safely begin again. It is too early to say that the CFP is a success, but it is certainly a great deal better than what might have happened.

It was a major achievement to reach agreement on a common policy, with majority voting prevailing on the details (as long as the Luxembourg Compromise is not invoked, as the Danes have done on several occasions). Otherwise there would have been a serious risk that the extension of fishery limits to 200 miles would have led to the sort of clashes which took place between Britain and Iceland in the Cod War of 1975. Mr Walker and Mr Buchanan-Smith, who with great difficulty carried the industry with them, showed a lot of political courage in making the deal.

The question of fisheries was one of the most difficult subjects in the Spanish entry negotiations, since the Spaniards have a huge fishing fleet and very few fish left in their waters. After great difficulty it was decided that the only possible way to proceed was not to have a transitional period for fish, to make some small concessions to Spain about increased quantities of hake that their fishermen can take in the waters of other Community members, to have a review of the situation in the middle of the existing twenty-year Common Fisheries Policy regulation, but to provide that things will go on as they are now until the year 2002 unless the Council decides otherwise. There are also provisions about the number of Spanish boats allowed to fish in the waters of the other members and some Community aid for scrapping Spanish boats.

This solution was in fact reasonably equitable in relation to the Common Fisheries Policy as adopted by the Ten. But the Spanish fishermen were disappointed and may try to push the Spanish government towards a renegotiation before the mid-term review in 1992. Let us hope not. It is highly unlikely to be possible to give Spanish fishermen more fish without other Community fishermen being given less.

Even the CFP is an area of national life which would now be hard to disentangle from the Community. Superficially it might seem simple to replace it with national arrangements! The UK could take back control of its own 200-mile limits and kick the Danes, the French, the Germans, the Irish, the Dutch, the Belgians and the Spaniards out of its waters. It could institute national conservation measures and take steps to enforce them. But in practice we should have to negotiate with all these countries about historic rights and we should have to replace Community control rules with national rules, compatible with the UK–EC fishing agreement which would no doubt need to be made. We should in any case need agreed conservation arrangements. To proceed without agreement would involve such serious quarrels and require such extensive and expensive fishery protection, to say nothing of risking a herring and mackerel war, that it could hardly be contemplated. The CFP has become a durable, if not popular, part of the national life.

THE ENVIRONMENT

The Treaty makes no provision for a common environment policy, which was a non-subject in the late 1950s. The environmental awakening began in the second half of the 1960s, leading to the creation of national administrations – in Britain the Department of the Environment was created in 1971. The Paris Summit of October 1972 included in its final Declaration the statement that harmonious development was not possible without an effective campaign to combat pollution and nuisances and that it was therefore necessary to implement a Community environment policy. Given that there was nothing about it in the Treaty, the common Action Programmes which have been undertaken since 1973 have been done under Article 100 (Approximation of Laws directly Affecting the Functioning of the Common Market) and Article 235 (the Article providing for common action where the necessary powers to attain one of the objectives of the Community have not been included in the Treaty). This is a good example of the pragmatic way in which the Community adds subjects to its agenda where necessary.

With each year that has passed, the environment has of course become an increasingly important subject from a political point of view, as well as in the natural world. With German forests dying and the ecology movement growing, what happens in the Environment Council has become a matter of high-level political concern.

The substance of Community discussions has always been extremely difficult, partly because of the different geographical situations of member states, partly because the political pressures were very different. It would not, for example, be reasonable to require exactly the same degree of purity in a river flowing into the Atlantic on the west coast of Ireland as in a tributary of the Rhine. On the other hand, certainly as far as air pollution is concerned, some member states are convinced that pollution generated in other member states is causing critically important damage in their countries.

The British have always been among those who press two general points strongly. First, any action to combat pollution ought to be based on scientific criteria, though they recognise that it is not possible to wait for absolute scientific proof if that means allowing irreversible damage to be done. Second, it is essential to weigh the environmental advantages of any course of action against the industrial and regulatory costs.

So far three Action Programmes have been adopted – 1973–77, 1977–81, and 1983–86. The first Programme began by laying down some general principles, including the principle of 'polluter pays', and went on to agree specific action to define quality objectives for, for example, different uses of water (drinking water, industry, etc.). In the second Programme, action to reduce and prevent water and atmospheric polution was included, as well as general action to protect and improve the environment. The third Programme, which extended and updated the second, included action to integrate the environmental dimension into other policies, action to reduce oxides of nitrogen and sulphur dioxide, and trans-frontier pollution, and action to reduce oil pollution at sea, including arrangements for handling and trans- porting dangerous substances and wastes.

Serious differences of opinion broke out in 1985 about the composition and levels of pollution in car exhaust emissions. Germany, intensely concerned about dying trees and subject to strong pressure from the Greens, pressed for a very low compulsory level, involving major expenditure by the car industry. Other member states producing cars, especially the UK, France and Italy, thought that they were going too far. After a difficult negotiation, a compromise was in the end achieved in the summer of 1984, though subject to a Danish reserve which has become entangled with the treaty amendment issue and which will not be lifted before the autumn of 1986.

The next important subject for discussion in the Council, and one which is perhaps even more difficult, is the control of emissions from industrial combustion plants. The action being proposed by the Commission is a target global reduction to be achieved by December 1995 of 60% for sulphur dioxide, 40% for nitrogen dioxide, and 40% for particulates. These proposals raise very serious questions, both about the scientific determination of the results of pollution caused by these plants and about the balance between the environmental advantages and the costs (which might amount to £1.5 billion for the UK alone).

The Environment is, of course, one of the great world issues of our time. What happens to the tropical rain forest, the oceans and the atmosphere will have more impact on the lives of our grandchildren than many of the issues which loom equally large today. European action is not a substitute for world action. But Europe is where we live, pollution generated in one European country can have devastating effects for another ande it is often easier for all to take expensive preventive or curative action together than to do it individually – with all the anxieties which arise about giving advantage to competitors. Above all, European Community legislation provides a ready-made vehicle for ensuring that action agreed among the governments is rapidly and fairly implemented. It is significant and encouraging that there was no disagreement among the Heads of Government in December 1985 about the principle of including a passage on the environment in the revision of the Treaty.

Even if the tide is flowing strongly in the direction of action to protect the environment, we can continue nevertheless to expect great controversy about the details of the measures to be applied. There will be the usual reports of Community rows. But we can also be sure that there will be a number of important agreements over the next few years. For it to be otherwise would be bad politics as well as bad sense everywhere in Europe.

RULES OF COMPETITION AND STATE AIDS

This is an area in which the Commission has been given important powers to be exercised directly under Articles 85–94 of the Treaty, for the very good reason that otherwise there would be a grave risk of the governments and industries in member states colluding to gain an unfair advantage. Articles 85 and 86 contain tough anti-monopoly, anti-cartel provisions, Article 92 bans state aids in principle, with some exceptions, though Article 93 gives the Commission discretion to find certain aids compatible with the Treaty. These rules lie at the heart of the free market approach in the Treaty of Rome. The founding fathers believed in the virtues of free competition and saw clearly how state aids can distort it.

All member governments are in constant and often tough negotiation with the Commission on the state aids front. A number of companies, including IBM, have had long and sometimes crucial negotiations on the competition front. The Commissioner in charge at present, Mr Sutherland, like his predecessor in the last Commission, Mr Andriessen, has been showing a marked determination to tighten up the application of the rules.

There is a strong case for rigorous interpretation of the Treaty by the Commission with, however, in my view, one exception. The creation of a world market for so many products like cars or computers makes it inappropriate to apply the rules as though European companies compete only with each other in the Community market. It does not make sense to forbid European companies to co-operate together on the grounds of reduction of competition in new high technology industries where the Americans and the Japanese are certainly going to produce more than enough competition to keep European industry on its toes for the foreseeable future.

State aids in the steel industry were dealt with in Chapter Three. Rather similar circumstances apply as regards shipbuilding where there is a Community Directive. The Commission are trying gradually to phase out aids for the textile and man-made fibres industries. On the other hand, they have put off any attempt to enforce a ban on aid for the coal industry on the unspoken, but sensible, grounds that it would not help the British or French Governments and their Coal Boards to persuade the trade unions to accept the restructuring of the industry if the Commission sought to enforce the ban on state aid provided for in the Treaty.

Other specific problems arise in other industries. The Commission which tries to take account of differing circumstances is sometimes criticized by purists for not taking a simple, absolutist line. On the whole, however, even German and British Ministers, who are the strongest supporters of applying the Treaty rigorously, find themselves on balance in favour of a sensibly flexible approach.

All aids have in principle to be notified to the Commission and, since the Commission has the power to authorise them or not, national officials and Ministers need to negotiate with the Commission about the conditions in which each aid may be given and its amount. It is relatively easy to be in favour of rigorous Commission action when state aids in other countries are involved. But most Ministers find themselves arguing from time to time for flexibility when their own are under discussion – not that all Ministers everywhere are entirely reconciled in their hearts to having to negotiate with the Commission before they can give their own government money to their own industries!

ECONOMIC AND MONETARY POLICY

Under Articles 103 and 104, member states are obliged to treat their macro-economic policy as a matter of common concern and to co-ordinate their economic and monetary policy. This work is carried out under the ECOFIN Council by the Monetary Committee on the one hand, and the Economic Policy Committee on the other. Community Central Bank governors also co-ordinate their policies. Member governments do in a sense genuinely regard each other's macro-economic policies as concerning all of them. What happens to the German economy, for example, is of crucial importance to a number of other countries. With every year that passes the economies become more integrated and interdependent.

The Community is still a long way from macro-economic policy-making in the Council. Finance, Economic and Budget Ministers do, however, take a lot more account now of the consequences of their actions for other Community countries than they did fifteen or twenty years ago. The EMS (see below) imposes quite a strict discipline on fiscal and monetary policy. But these things remain also the stuff of national politics and the balance is likely only to change slowly.

Capital movements should in principle be free, but countries such as France, Italy, and Belgium have always maintained exchange controls, with the Commission giving routine authorisation under Article 108. Minds are changing, however, and there is likely to be both quicker movement towards freeing up the capital markets and more stringent Commission control in future.

The Community has gone less far less quickly than was envisaged in the Treaty in these fields – and infinitely less far than the Paris 1972 Summit communiqué, which envisaged the creation of a full economic and monetary union (EMU) by 1980. This cautious approach is perhaps not surprising. Whatever the Heads of Government may have thought at the time about EMU, the finance ministries in almost all member states were deeply sceptical about a commitment to have it by 1980. They could see that, in order to implement it literally, including fixed parities or a single currency, giant strides would have to be made not only towards similar rates of inflation and productivity growth, but also towards sharing sovereignty in the fields of fiscal and monetary policy, giant strides for which political parties and electorates were totally unprepared – in both senses of the word, not warned and not willing.

Paradoxically, perhaps the most important action undertaken in the economic and monetary field has been taken outside the Treaty, namely the effort made by eight member states through the exchange rate mechanism (ERM) of the EMS to create a zone of monetary stability in Europe. The wide fluctuations of exchange rates which began after the breakdown of the Bretton Woods system in the early 1970s were deeply damaging to trade and investment in a steadily integrating European economy. No company can easily plan its sales and investments even for the coming year, let alone the long term, if exchange rates move 10% to 15% in a week and twice that in a year. There were therefore strong practical as well as Community reasons for trying to set up a European system which would tie the Community currencies as closely together as economic and monetary circumstances allowed.

This idea, foreshadowed in a speech by Mr Roy Jenkins as President of the Commission, was pushed forward by Chancellor Schmidt and President Giscard at the Copenhagen Summit in April 1978. Between that European Council and the Bremen European Council in July, the French and Germans invited the British to join for once in a tripartite enterprise to follow up Copenhagen and prepare an outline scheme for the next European Council in Bremen in July. Tripartite meetings between France, Germany and Britain are normally to be avoided in view of the trouble they cause with those who are left out! That being said, on this occasion we might have done well to join in with some zeal. Unfortunately we hung back in so clear a way that the French and Germans went ahead and produced proposals for Bremen on their own.

The Bremen communiqué carried the work considerably forward, with the Callaghan government in the last year of its life very hesitant indeed. In the early autumn, Mr Callaghan and Mr Healey decided that they would keep Britain out of any exchange rate mechanism (ERM) which might be established, though it would be desirable if possible to be a member of the European Monetary System itself. This quarter-in, three-quarters-out position was successfully negotiated when the EMS proposals were finally approved at the European Council in Brussels in December 1978. It was known in Whitehall as 'the soft landing' and there is no doubt that it was preferable to the hard landing of complete exclusion. But I continue to think that full membership would have been better for Britain at that time.

Since then, the Treasury and the government have been keeping the matter under review. In my own opinion, the present Government would have done well promptly to join the ERM on coming into office in the summer of 1979. But at that time, orthodox monetarists, among whom many Ministers counted themselves, believed in not having an exchange rate policy at all. The Treasury, who certainly never subscribed to this belief in any doctrinaire way, were hesitant about giving up the flexibility which a floating currency gives them. As the pound was strengthening by mid-1979 they no longer argued as they had under the Labour government, that joining the ERM would lead to an unacceptable loss of reserves; but switched instead to saying that holding the pound down against upward pressures would lead to Treasury loss of control over the money supply. This latter argument has always seemed to me to be flawed, but since it is no longer in the forefront of debate, it is perhaps not necessary to go into it here.

The EMS does not, of course, provide for a fixed-rate system like Bretton Woods. When necessary, governments have always been able to adjust their parity within the ERM after discussion between finance ministers. These discussions, usually held at the weekend, are naturally not always smooth, but on all occasions when finance ministers have met to discuss a realignment, agreement has been reached, sometimes after a bit of public drama. It would be extremely awkward to face the markets on Monday morning after a failure to agree!

Had Britain joined the ERM in 1979, there would no doubt have had to be one or two small revaluations of the pound during 1980–81. But a 10% revaluation in all might have been sufficient, had Britain been inside, as against the damaging peak of 25% revaluation which took place outside.

Of course, once the pound had risen to the exaggerated heights of 1980/82 outside the ERM, it would have been a grave mistake to join it. Whereas with a floating rate, a devaluation of 10% or even 15% could take place in quite a short time without any major political impact at home, there is no doubt that government decisions to make devaluations are politically difficult and damaging. Those in principle in favour of joining the ERM therefore had to bide their time.

During 1985, opinion moved rather strongly in the direction of joining, with the CBI and a number of important bankers coming out in favour. (The House of Commons Committee on the subject divided 5:4 against, but with some of the opponents influenced by the view that the current £–DM rate was too high.) What moved the bankers and industrialists was that well over 60% of our exports go to Community or EFTA countries whose currencies are formally or informally linked to the ECU. What industry wants above all else is stability.

In my own view, it remains highly desirable to join as soon as the conditions are ripe to permit us to hold the parity at which we join for a reasonably long period. It would be damaging politically to join one month and to be forced to devalue the next. The timing involves a difficult judgement which has to take politics as well as British and world economics into account. With the approach of the next British elections, which have to be held not later than the spring of

1988, and given the radically different economic policies being advocated by the Opposition, the pound could well be pushed downwards by speculative selling. Once inside the ERM the only options open to the Government would probably be devaluation or massive increases in interest rates. They would no doubt prefer to allow the exchange rate to float temporarily downwards.

When will the right time be? Some of the government's critics think that it will always find the time unripe. Personally, I hope and believe that this charge will prove unfounded. But it may not be until after the next elections.

This chapter needs to be rounded off with a passage on the ECU, an acronymic masterpiece derived from the specially invented 'European Currency Unit' (in fact, the Community's old unit of account before the ECU was called the European Unit of Account, EUA). It had the great merit of producing the name of an ancient and famous French coin. The ECU is made up of a basket of the Community currencies with each being given a weight broadly in proportion to the economic weight of the country concerned. It is used in the Community budget and for transactions between Central Banks under the EMS. It is the central point in the EMS currency grid. But, in addition, it has begun to take on a life of its own. Despite German unwillingness to regard the ECU as anything more than a unit of account, Governments and companies borrow in ECUs on the world's bond markets. The private individual in most Community countries can even have his traveller's cheques denominated in ECUs, though it is not yet all that easy to cash them! I would not be wholly surprised if, in my lifetime, the Community agreed to print ECU banknotes alongside pounds, francs and marks – but very surprised if it were to replace them.

There is a lot in a name. Very few people, except the experts, have even heard of the IMFs much older currency unit, the SDR. Would the ECU have caught on if it had gone on being called the EUA?

The linguistic connoisseur can take pleasure in the fact that a dispute broke out recently between the French and the Germans about whether the ECU, which is to be mentioned in a new Treaty article in a section oddly titled 'Monetary capacity', should be masculine or feminine in the German text. Is it a unit of account or an old French coin? I am not pulling the reader's leg.

In Chapters Two, Three and Four I have tried to say enough about a cross-section of the Community's agenda to enable the reader to understand why the Community is dealing with these subjects and what it is doing about them – the CAP, the internal market, industry, technology and research, fisheries, environment, competition and state aids, and economic and monetary policy.

This list does not make any attempt to be comprehensive. Some will certainly question the choice of subjects to be treated rather more fully. The work on harmonizing VAT; the tripartite meetings between industry, the trades unions and the governments on employment policy; the work on company law, product liability, insurance, banking practices, transport infrastructure or lorry weights; energy policy where much work has been done and where there are, for example, a number of significant demonstration projects in various fields of renewable energy sources; the work on 'social engineering' for example, parental leave, part-time working or Equal Opportunity legislation; the provision of loans under the European Investment Bank or the so-called Ortoli facility which permits the Commission itself to borrow on capital markets and to lend for specific purposes. All these subjects seem to those closely concerned to be high on the list of priorities from the point of view of their own lives or businesses. They are indeed intrinsically important. But if this book is to stand any chance of carrying the general reader with it to the end, it must not be overweighted with discussion of particular issues. That is why I have restricted my list and given the subjects dealt with simplified treatment. The aim is to illustrate the working of the Community with examples rather than to give a complete description of the subjects on its agenda.

5

The Council at Work

In CONSTITUTIONAL THEORY, there is only one Council; in practice, there are many (see Chapter Two). *Primus inter pares*, below the European Council (Heads of Government), is the General Affairs Council on which Foreign Ministers sit. It deals with constitutional questions and many of the more important internal policies, such as, for example, the Regional Fund or the Own Resources Decision as well as the main issues in the Community's relations with the rest of the world. It is the Council in charge of co-ordinating the rest of the Community's work as well as preparing the European Council (Heads of Government). Though the other 'specialist' Councils, which deal with one or more specific subjects, have slightly different personalities, the basic working methods are not so very different.

The Foreign Ministers know each other well, communicate with each other easily (almost all have some common language), and many of them like each other. There is a genuine feeling of a Foreign Ministers' club.

The ministers meet collectively in Brussels about twelve times a year for Council meetings, in the capital of the Presidency once or twice each six months, at the time of the United Nations' General Assembly, and often when they are all together for other international meetings. They spend two informal weekends together a year. They meet bilaterally a great deal – say fifteen or twenty meetings a year for each minister.

One might think that, in these circumstances, they would be able to settle things rather quickly when they meet. But it is not so easy. In Political Co-operation, where the Foreign Minister is normally the only minister in his national government to have responsibility and where spending money is seldom involved, it is easier than in the Council where the opposite usually applies. But even in Political Co-operation there are factors working against easy consensus. The Greeks, for example, for home political reasons, would much rather not take a common position with the major West European countries on East-West or Arab-Israeli questions and no one else feels the way

73

they do about the Turks. For Ireland, it would be politically damaging to do anything which could be taken to mean they were moving nearer to NATO. For the Danes, there are questions on which it is painful for them politically to separate themselves from the other Scandinavians. Denmark and Greece are unable, for quite different reasons, to take a relaxed view about the human rights situation in Turkey. For France, during 1985, it seemed good politics to get ahead of others in being tough with South Africa. And so on.

Another problem is caused by jockeying for political advantage either at home or with the governments of other countries. If the one Foreign Minister judges that another minister or ministers will refuse to agree to a plan to give additional aid, say, to Central America, he may be tempted to propose or support it (even if he does not much want it to happen) so that the foreign government concerned and/or his national parliament (if it is a popular cause) can be told that he has proposed it but that it could not be agreed. Of course, it is not possible to prove that a minister is playing games of this kind. The minister concerned would no doubt say that his country really wanted the action to be taken, and would wax indignant at the idea that anyone could suggest he was playing games. All the same, a lot of games do get played!

But the central reason why the Council is slow to take its decisions is that it can only decide when the national governments are ready to decide. Most decisions about the internal affairs of the Community, whether it be, for example, the arrangements for distributing money from the Regional Fund or spending money on the Community's research programmes, involve several ministries in every capital. Everybody knows that, in the end, agreement has got to be reached; but equally that a tough negotiation is going to take place beforehand. So, when officials or ministers meet in capitals to decide on the brief for the Council at the beginning of the debate on a subject, they adopt a maximalist line. They know that they have to make concessions later but, equally, that they will not get a good deal if they do not ask for a lot at the beginning and stick to it for quite a long time.

Among the member states, other than Britain, the French are the arch negotiators. (Many in Brussels would bracket Britain and France together in that category.) I have long suspected that there must be a negotiating manual somewhere in the French machine because their negotiators so often seem to follow the same pattern. They take a very hard line for months. The time approaches when they judge that a decision is going to be taken soon. They soften on some minor points and indicate a readiness to negotiate. However, just before the crunch meeting, their line hardens and two or three points which have scarcely appeared in their speeches before suddenly assume great prominence. They announce that they cannot possibly move on them.

Their adversaries in the negotiation do well to try to put themselves in the French shoes. If these new points are worth money to the French or if they seem likely to be important politically in France, they may be real sticking-points. But, far more often, they are discards, points which have been blown up specially so that they can be elegantly abandoned at two in the morning on the last day, while preserving the things that really matter in France's original position.

One of the troubles about taking a tough line early in a negotiation is that everything which is said in the Council becomes known to the press (though the Council is not of course open to press or public), even if the minister concerned does not himself tell the journalists – and normally they do. The news-sheet published every day in Brussels, called *Agence-Europe*, has sources which enable it to give broadly accurate accounts of Commission, COREPER and Council meetings within a day or two of them taking place. So the hardline negotiating position becomes known, the minister is questioned about it in his own parliament and he cannot, of course, say that his hard line is only a negotiating position. The Opposition have every interest in pinning him to it so that he appears to have negotiated weakly when he makes concessions. It becomes more difficult for him to make them.

And there is another problem. Let us assume that the question under negotiation involves expenditure. Most governments, but especially the British, German and, to some extent, French Governments, which are the major net contributors to the Community, have trouble in persuading their finance ministries to agree to spend still more money even on worthy causes. Let us assume that one or more of them adopt an opening position which is rigorously opposed to new expenditure, which is often the case. The finance ministry will then have every interest in holding the government as hear to its original negotiating position as it can. This can cause serious delays. The Germans, for example, are notoriously slow to coordinate changes in their negotiating position, once adopted, and often they become matters of coalition politics.

All that being said, it is nevertheless the case that all Foreign Ministers know that, on almost every issue, they have got to agree in the end. They are condemned to achieve a successful outcome to a Community negotiation, even if they have sometimes made it difficult for themselves to present success in the Community other than as a failure at home.

The Foreign Affairs Council generally meets on Monday, usually starting with an informal working lunch in the Charlemagne Building where the meeting takes place. There are three big conference rooms on the 15th Floor, arranged so that there are forty to fifty places at 'the table', in fact a large open rectangle. The President, with the Secretary-General and his advisers on one side and his Presidency delegation on the other, sits facing the Commission with the member states down the other two sides. The country holding the Presidency has separate national representation which has even been known to disagree with the President. Behind the front table, there is a second row where another sixty or so advisers can sit. Each delegation has three seats in the front row, each seat with earphones to provide interpretation into all the Community languages, and a microphone which is only switched on when the speaker has the floor. The interpreters sit in glass-fronted booths on two sides of the room. As in the House of Commons or any other large assembly, meetings in this room often look disorderly, more so than they are. People come and go. Advisers change as the agenda items change. People stand about and hold private conversations. From time to time an exasperated President stops the proceedings and restores quiet, perhaps insisting that all those without a seat shall leave the room.

On this floor, there is also a small conference room which holds only one or two per delegation, and where ministers are much closer to each other at a smaller oval table. They meet here in restricted session. It is an odd psychological fact that it is much easier to engage in an informal and effective negotiation in the small room with fewer people present.

On the 14th floor below, each delegation has a suite of three or four offices where ministers can be briefed by their staff; bilateral meetings can be held with other ministers; officials can draft speaking notes and telegrams; calls can be made to home capitals on the five or six telephones; and if there is a pause in the middle of the night, there is even a comfortable chair in which the minister can rest for a moment. It is not unknown for three Councils to take place on the same day, in which case the offices are noisy and overcrowded, and it is extremely difficult to get hold of a telephone. I remember a day when there were seven ministers in the British Government in Brussels and, naturally, I did not even manage to see them all.

Sir Geoffrey Howe normally arrives by RAF plane about an hour before the informal Council lunch and holds a briefing meeting. By that time, he and the London team of three or four officials and the Permanent Representative and his staff will have read the briefs for the meeting. The briefs set out the government's agreed objectives for each item, describe the objectives of other member states (partly derived from reports from Brussels, partly as a result of approaches by Embassies in Community capitals the week before), suggest a possible line to take for the minister, and provide a background note explaining the issues at stake. Very often, an item remains on the agenda of the Council several months running while slow progress is made towards the final negotiating crunch. Sir Geoffrey Howe is usually familiar with the subject already.

The briefing meeting does not therefore need to go into each subject in depth. The Permanent Representative and his staff report on the latest developments over the weekend and how the Chairman is being briefed to handle each item. The Chairman, incidentally, receives a handling brief from the Secretary-General as well as his own officials and a well-run Presidency will wish to ensure that delegations know how he is going to handle the meeting.

Normally the Permanent Representative, at least in the British case, has had a chance to look at the briefing in draft on the previous Friday. But occasionally he or his staff may think that there is a better approach than that set out in the line to take, and recommend it at the briefing meeting. If the minister agrees, someone redrafts it during the lunch-hour.

The Minister, the Permanent Representative, and one or two others go down to the Council lunch at 1.15 and, during the fifteen or twenty minutes before ministers go into lunch, quite a lot of lobbying of other delegations and the Commission goes on. The ministers eat on their own (with interpreters) and the Chairman normally plans to get quite a lot of business done over lunch. This also provides an occasion for more informal discussions about how the problems of the day might get solved. It is not always easy to hear what is going on at these lunches, with several interpreters whispering in ministers' ears, and misunderstandings about what has happened are not unknown. The normal practice, therefore, is that, where the Chairman has been able to sum up that something is agreed, he should nevertheless bring the matter to the formal Council, often with a short written conclusion prepared by the Secretary-General, and thus have it formally endorsed.

The Council, when it meets formally after lunch, first adopts the agenda which may have from six to twelve items on it, such as (a random sample) negotiations between the Commission and the United States about steel exports to America, the Spanish and Portuguese share of the Regional Fund, a ban on the import of seals from Canada, the tariff on video sets from Japan, the preparation of the next European Council, easing frontier controls, an increase in the duty-free allowance for travellers, and (separately and not on the formal agenda) perhaps a couple of political co-operation items such as South Africa and Central America.

The Council then approves the 'A' points without discussion. These may be important but they have been fully negotiated already, perhaps mainly at the last Council, and COREPER has since put the final touches to the drafting. If any delegation still has diffficulties with an 'A' point, it is simply withdrawn and COREPER sorts out the problems before the next Council. 'A' points need not necessarily deal with questions on the agenda of the Council which is meeting and can be taken at a Council meeting where no minister deals with the subject. Approving 'A' points is a purely formal act.

The Council then looks at the resolutions passed by the European Parliament at its last Session. The chairman draws its attention to the most significant ones and occasionally a minister comments. In principle, those resolutions should be fully taken into account at all stages of the discussion of each subject. In practice they are often ignored. The Council is committed to improving its performance in this respect.

The chairman needs to have a clear idea of what he wants to do on each item. If it is a new point, he will normally ask all those who want to speak to give their views and then, if there is already some degree of consensus, attempt to sum up with a few broad conclusions before remitting the matter for further work by COREPER. If it is something which has been discussed at several Councils already and only one or two delegations had difficulties with the majority view at the last meeting, the chairman will turn the pressure on those delegations to agree. Occasionally, if the question comes under a majority voting article of the Treaty, he will call for a vote. (The question of majority voting is dealt with separately in a later chapter.) Often the final decision is taken on the basis of a presidency (or Commission) compromise proposal.

Ministers themselves do not sit all the time. Herr Genscher, for example, was seldom present except for the more important discussions, leaving his deputy, then Herr Ruhfus (ex-German Ambassador in London) to defend the German cause on some of the issues.

Ministers have very different styles. M. Dumas, a brilliant ex-lawyer, almost always appeared to speak without a note and presented even a case which others did not agree with in a persuasive way. But when he became Foreign Minister (and no longer Minister for Europe), with so many other responsibilities, he too often left his deputy, Mme Lalumière, to speak for France.

Signor Andreotti of Italy is one of the oldest hands. Known, I believe, in Italy as 'Il Furbo' – the Cunning One – he was an effective President of the Foreign Affairs Council in the first half of 1985. Though no longer young, he appeared to have immense powers of endurance and, during the final stages of the Spanish and Portuguese enlargement negotiations, thought nothing of working most of the night several days running.

The President needs to have great patience. Very often he will know or sense that the minister who is making the most difficulties on a given question has to be seen at home to fight very hard before he compromises, or that he has authority to make a concession only if he finds himself isolated. So the President must give him time to fight the good fight. He must detach his allies one by one by offering unimportant, even verbal, concessions. And then at the appropriate time, sometimes far into the night, he will circulate the final presidency compromise proposal and try to rush it through. It is a mistake to circulate such a proposal too soon because then several other ministers may join in criticizing it and the discussion may start all over again.

The press always plays an important role in Council meetings though they are not, of course, present in the room except for the photographers at the very beginning. (These, incidentally, take several thousand photographs of the same people each month which has always seemed to me to be an uneconomic proposition.) But the press journalists and radio and television men are down on the ground floor and expect ministers to come and see them at least once during a meeting. Sir Geoffrey Howe will normally give them an on-the-record briefing before he has to go. If Sir Geoffrey Howe knows that he has to go before the main issues of business have been completed or if he is unable to come to a Council meeting, his deputy, the Minister of State in the Foreign Office, represents him.

It is important that at least half the delegations as well as the Presidency should be represented by ministers in order to avoid the risk of not having a quorum, without which no formal decisions can be taken. But ministers may, if they choose, leave their Permanent Representative to speak on their behalf and, once the Council is well-launched, one or two delegations are usually represented by them.

With a good brisk chairman and proper preparation, a lot can get settled at a Council. It is best when the Presidency and the key delegations concerned with the difficult items have done a lot of quiet work behind the scenes on compromise formulae. But without these favourable conditions, or if the problems involved are particularly intractable, the meetings can drag on far into the night. If the agenda is heavy, the Council will in any case have to continue on the following day. It is alleged that some delegations find it easier to settle in the middle of the night because it is not then possible to ring up their own President or Prime Minister. This may sometimes be a consideration, but not often. More usually, the meetings go on because the President hopes to wear the other ministers down. This can be an incredibly boring and tiresome process.

The Foreign Secretary's presence at the Council sometimes placed a strain on ambassadorial family life. Lord Carrington, Mr Pym and Sir Geoffrey Howe were all perfect guests, but they could do nothing about the unpredictability of Council life. I could never tell my wife whether we should be six or eight for dinner at 9.00 p.m. (or 11.00 p.m. for that matter), or whether we should be eating sandwiches in the Council. Equally, it was impossible to predict when we should come home to bed, if ever.

Painful though I have made it sound, I think that most ministers and officials do, however, enjoy the Council when things go well, when they get their way to a reasonable extent, and when a conclusion satisfactory to all can be drawn. But there is nothing more depressing than a Council at which, on four or five of the main items, the Chairman finally has to say: 'I do not think that we can get further here tonight. It is clear that there is no basis for agreement. The question will go back to COREPER and we will take it up again next month.'

The European Council is very different from the Foreign Ministers' Council. Though the Heads of Government see each other quite often, at three meetings of the Council a year (two from now on), at bilateral meetings, at Economic Summits, at Russian funerals, and so on, they know each other much less well than the Foreign Ministers. Many more of them are without a common language. They call each other by their Christian names, but it sometimes sounds a little odd. There is usually someone around to interpret in pauses in the meetings, gatherings over drinks before dinner, and so on. But communication through interpretation is not at all the same as a private and informal conversation.

When problems have failed to get settled lower down it usually means that they are intrinsically quite difficult. The Community has a way of complicating difficult problems as it tries to grind forward towards a solution. So the subject matter at meetings of the European Council is often unattractive and difficult to grasp.

Moreover, the European Council is to a still greater extent a media affair. Up to a thousand journalists come to the place where it is going on, although they seldom see the Heads of Government before the end. Dramas are always predicted, sometimes fabricated, but only too often provided.

By convention, there is no formal agenda. The Chairman normally writes to his colleagues a few days before the meeting and suggests the subjects which he thinks should be discussed. But it is not unknown for this or that Head of Government to spring something on the meeting without preparation.

It is the task of the Foreign Ministers to prepare the meetings. But the degree of preparation is very much a matter of the taste and tactics of the Presidency. Some Presidencies have tried a long and careful preparatory process, as the British did on the so-called 30th May Mandate in the autumn of 1981, or Greece did before the Athens Summit in December 1983. Neither of these meetings was successful. The French, on the other hand, only engaged in minimal preparation of their two European Councils in the first half of 1984, and scored a partial success in March and a relatively full success at Fontainebleau in June. But it would not be right to assume that it is always best to try to bounce people.

However sketchy or extensive the collective preparations of the European Council may be, Mrs Thatcher's own briefing is always full and comprehensive, often too much so, as she is liable to complain. There is a steering brief which tries to tell her the things which she does not know already about all the subjects which are certainly going to come up. On the day before the meeting, there is a full briefing session with the key ministers and officials concerned with all these subjects. Very often, during the days immediately before the meeting or at the briefing session itself, she will commission revised speaking notes on some of the subjects. And finally, in the plane on the way to the meeting, she likes to run through the agenda and her speaking notes and put in her handbag a few bits of paper containing key facts and points which she wants to make.

Some of the Heads of Government turn up with huge teams of advisers, twenty to thirty, or even more, which seems a lot given the fact that none of them are allowed to accompany their Head of Government into the Conference Room. The British were always a relatively small team, but Mrs Thatcher has insisted on pruning it still further. One or other member of this small team will know the answer to most questions the Prime Minister wants answered and if none of them do they can telephone to London.

Two of the three meetings each year were in the country of the Presidency, not always in the capital. For example, the Italians held their last meeting in the Sforza castle in Milan, and the French theirs in the château at Fontainebleau. (Now that it has been decided only to have two meetings in future, it will no doubt be the Brussels meeting, where the third was held, which will be dropped.)

A room is rigged up for the Heads of Government with a smallish hollow square table seating two per country, plus the President of the Commission. Only the Presidency and the Secretariat-General of the Council have officials in the room, at a small table behind the chair. But each Head of Government has a bell which rings in an ante-room where the so-called 'Antici' group sit. This group, named after its Italian founder long ago, normally is responsible for the detailed timing and organisation of COREPER and Council meetings under the direction of the Presidency and COREPER. At the European Council, its members act as a channel of communication between the Heads of Government and their advisers.

Mrs Thatcher and Sir Geoffrey Howe often press their bell – to send out notes asking for information or Sir Geoffrey's record of what takes place. Sometimes they call in the Permanent Representative or a Private Secretary for a brief, whispered consultation.

European Council meetings normally begin with a lunch. Much organisation is required to get all the planes to arrive in an agreed order. There is usually a Guard of Honour and a large motorcycle escort to whirl the Heads of Government to the meeting-place.

It is rare for much work to get done at lunch. So the real business begins with the formal session on the first afternoon and there is often some quiet procedural jockeying for position. Those Heads of Government who want a conclusion on a given subject press for it to be taken on the first day, knowing that otherwise there will be insufficient time for negotiation and the drafting of agreed texts. Mrs Thatcher often had trouble getting the British budget problem taken on the first day during the five years that the campaign went on.

The meetings go on until 7.00 or 7.30 p.m. and then there is a brief pause before dinner at which the Heads of Government dine alone in one room and the Foreign Ministers in another – and a buffet is provided for the hundreds of advisers in some vast hall. Mrs Thatcher always has a debriefing session with her team of advisers, both after the afternoon meeting and after the Heads of Government dinner at which some collective discussion usually takes place. Quite often, she would return from dinner around midnight or a little later, and there would then be a lively discussion about what to do next, sometimes lasting into the small hours. I remember that, at Stuttgart in the summer of 1983, it was 2.30 in the morning when she decided that she wanted a draft speaking note prepared for the next day. She instructed me to go to work and parade with the draft at 7.00 a.m.!

Overnight, the Presidency normally prepares draft conclusions, certainly on the subjects which have been discussed, and sometimes on ones which have not. The latter are liable to give rise to trouble when submitted to the Heads of Government! The British member of the Antici Group picks these drafts up early in the morning and the official team quickly annotate copies for the Prime

Minister and the Foreign Secretary so that they are aware of the problems and ready with amendments, if necessary.

After a 'family photograph' of the Heads of Government and their Foreign Secretaries, the Council resumes between 9.00 and 10.00 a.m. It often has not completed the first round of discussion of the agenda and frequently has some difficult conclusions to negotiate. There always seems to be time pressure. Some Heads of Government announce that they have to leave at a certain time in the afternoon, and some of them mean it. More often it is a negotiating ploy or designed to make the Presidency get a move on.

When the negotiations get really difficult, the Presidency usually calls a pause every hour or two so that Heads of Government can consult their advisers and talk to each other informally. One or two Heads of Government, often including President Mitterrand, sit quietly at the table, seeming relatively detached from what is going on. Others are talking to their advisers or to potential allies in the negotiation. The President bustles around from group to group, trying to push his colleagues towards a solution. Sometimes, as at Stuttgart or Milan, quite heated discussions break out. Not everybody always understands what is going on. Scenes such as this, involving the President of France and nine (now eleven) Prime Ministers could not take place anywhere else. There is an informality, even intimacy, which is a world away from the formality of normal international life at this level.

Some Presidencies have kept the Heads of Government sitting at the negotiating table far into the afternoon without lunch, possibly on the theory that hunger will be an inducement to compromise. My observation has been that the consequence is, on the contrary, that the Heads of Government become irritable and that they are much more likely to settle if they break for a short lunch before 2.00 p.m.

Whether the meetings end in success or failure depends to quite a large degree on the timing. It is rare for Heads of Government to be prepared to slog on much after 6.00 or 7.00 p.m. in the evening on the second day (though they went on till midnight in Luxembourg in December 1985 in order not to go home without agreement on Treaty changes). So, if the Chairman cannot get the main problems solved by 3.00 or 4.00 p.m., allowing two hours for clearing up drafting points and agreeing conclusions on subsidiary matters, he may well find that he simply has to conclude that nothing can get settled that day.

It is an odd way for the great men and women of Europe to do business. Very often a number of them, particularly if they are relatively new in office and have not been Foreign Secretary before, find the whole process hard to understand and the subject matter difficult to grasp. Quite often, the Council

83

finds itself arguing over points of drafting because it is the details of the conclusions which matter, sometimes involving very substantial sums of money.

No Head of Government can get his or her way unless prepared to argue points of detail and to keep on insisting that the necessary amendments to the Presidency draft under discussion be made. Even more than in other Community negotiations those who get their way are those who know their subject, know exactly what they want and are determined to get it.

I am conscious that this description is rather abstract, without specific examples of the discussions. I thought of trying to include a few examples from recent years such as the negotiations on wine at Dublin (Winter 1984) or on Integrated Mediterranean Programmes at Brussels (Spring 1985). But the exposition required to make the description of the negotiation comprehensible would have been too long.

So it seemed to me that the practical thing to do was to treat separately the five-year-long negotiation about the British budget contribution, so much of which took place at successive European Councils. The budget story needs to be told somewhere, at least in summary form, and it will serve to illustrate how the European Council actually works.

6

The Community Budget and Resource Transfers

THE COMMUNITY BUDGET is neither like a national budget nor like that of an ordinary international organisation. Unlike national budgets, it remains insignificant in terms of macro-economic policy, less than 1% of GDP compared with the 40% or more of GDP which is consumed by national budgets. To say this is not to argue that the sums involved are small in relation to other things on which the money could be spent. But it offers no scope in terms of demand management.

On the other hand, it is quite unlike the budget of, say, NATO or the United Nations. There are no fixed percentage contributions. And a large part of Community expenditure cannot be fixed in advance, because for the CAP i.e., 70% of the budget, the actual sum spent in any given year is broadly determined by previous decisions by the Agriculture Council and considerably affected by the harvest and the level of world prices, but not at all by the figure written into the budget. Furthermore, the Council and the Parliament, the two halves of the budgetary authority, both play an important part in fixing the total budget as well as its component parts and seldom work together in a rational way.

Under the Own Resources Decision of 1970, revised in 1985, the proceeds of all agricultural levies and duties and industrial tariffs (less a 10% collection charge) are paid over to the Community automatically. In addition, the Commission is entitled to call up a percentage of member states' VAT, up to a limit of 1% under the 1970 decision, increased to 1.4% in 1985, in order to meet the expenditure in the budget. (The VAT in question is not that actually paid over to the national governments – because they levy the tax on different things. A notional VAT base has been agreed and the payments to the Community are based on that.)

By the time the increase in the VAT ceiling to 1.4% was at last approved in 1985, expenditure was in fact running at about 1.1%. Since the British rebate agreed at Fontainebleau (see next chapter) will cost the others at least 0.1% of

VAT from the 1986 budget onwards, only 0.2% extra was in theory available for meeting the costs of enlargement (Spain and Portugal), of integrated Mediterranean programmes, of new policies in the fields of technology, research, etc. Alas, the CAP has eaten most of this up already. But it will not be easy to increase the ceiling again.

Most Community governments are fighting hard to contain government expenditure as a whole. Increasing the VAT paid over to the Community is therefore unpopular with finance ministers, even those whose countries hope to draw increased net benefits; extremely unpopular in the net contributor countries, Germany, Britain, and now France. Every 0.1% of VAT which goes to Brussels is 0.1% less for the national budget.

In 1984 and 1985, while the new Own Resources Decision was under discussion, it proved impossible to contain the budget within the 1% ceiling and in each of those years member governments agreed to a special additional contribution of a billion ECUs or more through an *ad hoc* intergovernmental agreement. For Britain this was difficult once, and only supportable twice because it was an integral part of the package under which a long-term settlement to the British budget problem was agreed. Now that CAP costs have risen above the strict financial guideline, there will be those in other countries who argue for a third such agreement to meet commitments to farmers already entered into. The British Government and Parliament will be hard to persuade either to raise the ceiling or to provide more *ad hoc* finance, despite the indication (without commitment) in the Fontainebleau agreement that a further increase to 1.6% might be made in 1988.

It must not, however, be forgotten that, Britain's substantial rebate on its VAT payments under the Fontainebleau agreement will have the effect of keeping the British VAT percentage well below 1% while others move up to the 1.4%. So there will no doubt be pressure on the UK from most, perhaps all, the other member governments not to block the provision of more money to keep the CAP going. Quite soon it will be necessary to start to think about the negotiating position in those circumstances.

Germany will also get a small rebate under the Fontainebleau agreement, so that the burden of financing the British rebate bears slightly less heavily on them. The result, combined with the rapid increase in CAP expenditure outside France, has been to turn France into a major net contributor together with Germany (now, by far, the biggest) and Britain. Indeed, the French will now be overtaking the British. All the rest remain net beneficiaries (though Belgium would be a net contributor if the administrative expenses of the

Commission did not count as benefits to Belgium under the Commission's method of calculation). The fact that France, Germany and Britain will be the major net contributors is bound to affect the way in which the two groups look at Community policies in the years to come.

There are already signs of an important forthcoming clash of interests between the less prosperous – Greece, Ireland, Spain, Portugal – who are demanding an increase in resource transfers in order to make possible a convergence in economic performance between the two groups – and the richer net contributors, who feel that they are doing quite enough already, at least for Ireland (which gets more than 5% of its GNP from the Community budget) or Greece, whose net benefits are now almost 1,000 million ECUs annually. But Portugal, far poorer, will only receive 200–300 million ECUs and Spain is unlikely to do much better than break even in the first four years of membership.

Apart from the CAP, of which the resource transfer effects are arbitrary (Denmark, the richest member, being a major net beneficiary), the main vehicles for resource transfers to the less rich are the Regional and Social Funds and, now for a few years, the integrated Mediterranean programmes, of which Greece will be the main beneficiary.

Paradoxically, since Britain is probably about to become a net contributor to a vastly increased Regional Fund, its origins can be found in the 1971 entry negotiations about the prospective British net contribution to the Community budget. The British were told that their budgetary problem would disappear as other Community policies of benefit to Britain developed. So the Heath Government looked around for ways of increasing Community expenditure in the UK and its eye came to rest on Britain's regional problems. At the 1972 and 1973 Paris and Copenhagen Summits, Mr Heath put his major negotiating effort into getting agreement to the Regional Fund and in the end succeeded on a modest scale.

From the start, therefore, the British Treasury regarded it as a means of channelling Community money back into the UK. Ireland, by far the poorest member state in those days, and Italy, because of the *Mezzogiorno*, also saw it as an ideal way of channelling additional Community money into their countries. No one in any of the Community governments contemplated creating a centralised Community regional policy with the Commission allocating available funds in accordance with its views of the objective needs of problem areas. So there was no choice but to have a disagreeable negotiation about national quotas for regional expenditure.

The French fought hard to avoid becoming net contributors. The Irish and the Italians, both incidentally countries with an excellent record of success in promoting their national interests in the Community, pointed with justice to the poverty of large areas in their countries. British representatives fought their own corner hard. The results were a major success for Italy, which secured just over 40% of the fund, a satisfactory additional source of Community income for Ireland with about 6% and a modest success for the UK at about 27%. These figures have naturally to be seen in relation to each country's share of gross contributions, percentages which vary a little from year to year with exchange rate movements and so on. On this, the real basis, Italy did exceptionally well, taking home about 27% of the fund net; Ireland secured a net gain of over 5%, substantial in later years in relation to Irish GNP, and Britain about 7%, declining after 1976 as our exchange rate rose. (This meant, of course, that regional expenditure could never have any appreciable effect on a UK net contribution of 2 billion ECUs or more, since even in the best year 1 billion ECUs of regional expenditure would only have yielded a net gain of 70 million for the UK.)

The Fund started modestly, but grew rapidly to about 950 million ECUs in 1979 and, with the help of the European Parliament, to nearly 2,400 million ECUs in 1984. The money was spent in accordance with certain agreed rules, largely at least in the case of the UK replacing government or local authority expenditure. It is hard to say how much Community expenditure has been 'additional' to what would have been spent otherwise. Who can ever say what would have happened otherwise? The British Government naturally takes account, in fixing its regional expenditure plans, of the likely contribution from the Regional Fund.

There have been several important negotiations about the Fund since 1974. When it was renewed in 1979, 5% of expenditure was taken off-quota and the Commission given discretion on how to spend it, within agreed guidelines. Then the accession of Greece in 1981 brought in another candidate for net benefits. After a tough negotiation, Greece secured a reasonable share at about 15%, bringing all other quotas down in consequence, that of the UK to under 24% (and a net gain of about 3%). In 1984, the Regional Fund regulation was revised and the straight quotas were replaced by a minimum/maximum percentage range, thus giving the Commission a greater degree of discretion (11% compared to 5% for the non-quota section). The UK fought hard and successfully to retain regions in industrial decline on an equal footing with regions in need of development as beneficiaries of the Fund. With the accession of Spain and Portugal, a new negotiation about quota ranges will have to take place. It is hard to see how Britain can hope to secure a deal which still leaves us as a net beneficiary.

Except as a channel for transferring resources from the richer to the poorer member states, the Regional Fund has few merits. Member governments have a poor record of publicising the Community's contribution to projects partly financed by it (under the rules this cannot normally be more than 50%). In many cases the government concerned would have undertaken the expenditure itself if there had been no Regional Fund. It is not a real Community policy in the sense of achieving common aims or taking joint action and the Community as such gains few advantages from it.

Unlike the Regional Fund, the Social Fund is based on the Treaty (Articles 123-128). It operates in two broad fields: training and job creation, in accordance with guidelines drawn up by the Commission. Forty per cent of the Fund has been reserved for super-priority areas such as Ireland, Northern Ireland, Greece, and the *Mezzogiorno*. The Commission have considerable but not unlimited discretion about how the money is spent. An important factor in determining where the money is spent has been the skill (and timing) of applications in relation to the rules.

The Social Fund too has grown rapidly– to a total of nearly 1900 million ECUs in 1984. British local authorities have been skilful in devising schemes for training and for helping companies to employ young people. Britain has therefore done well out of the Fund, getting about 28% of the expenditure on average over the past few years. But here, too, it will be hard for Britain to remain a net beneficiary, given the very strong case for Spanish and, especially, Portuguese net benefits.

President Delors is not satisfied with the present operation of the funds and may get the Commission to improve the co-ordination of expenditure from them. Their future may also well become tied up with the debate about what volume of resources should flow from North to South, from richer to poorer, in the Community. For the time being, and probably the time being will prove lasting, the net contributors will be most reluctant to concede any further point of principle on this point and in practice will seek to channel any increase in transfers to Portugal and to a lesser extent Spain rather than Greece, Ireland or Italy.

The only other major expenditures financed by the budget (apart from administration costs) are food aid and research and development, the latter now 1000m ECUs a year and rising. With the solution to the UK budget problem behind us (see next chapter), we hear no more about there being a goal of constant expansion of Community expenditure on new policies. Few of the governments ever really believed in this – though some people in the Commission may have done. Even in the prosperous Sixties there was no tendency to undertake Community expenditure lightly. In recent years the budget has been under the same sort of pressure as national budgets and – leaving aside the argument about the CAP – there is now little fat in it.

Alas, as Chapter 2 showed, the CAP is quite capable, on its own, of using up all the existing 'own resources' within the 1.4% ceiling – and no doubt a lot more too, if the governments were to allow it. Sanity cannot return to the Community budget scene until the cost of the CAP is, by one means or another, brought under control.

7

The British Budget Problem

THE SCALE OF the prospective British net contribution to the Community budget – the difference between what Britain pays in to the Community and the Community pays out in Britain to implement Community policies – caused difficulties in the entry negotitions in 1971. It was the main subject in the 'renegotiation' of the terms of entry in 1974/75 and it bedevilled Britain's relations with the other member states during the first five years of the present Conservative Government. Was all this necessary and inevitable?

This question has to be answered against the political background of the 1970s. The anti-marketeer critics of British membership were then quite strong. The sums of money involved were considerable. £1,000 million may be only a fraction of 1% of British GNP, but it is significant in terms of other government expenditure which need not be squeezed if the money does not have to flow out to Brussels. The decisive factor was, however, the political impossibility of defending a completely inequitable situation. Why should Britain, by 1970 already much less rich, in terms of GNP per head, than France, Denmark or the Netherlands, be so heavy a net contributor while they were big net beneficiaries?

The need to be able to argue that the entry terms were fair therefore ensured that the problem had to be raised in the entry negotiations; the fact that only a vague general assurance and a long transitional period could be secured in the entry negotiations meant that the issue had to be at the centre of 're-negotiation', and the failure to secure an effective correction in 1975 resulted in a rapidly rising net contribution as the transitional period came to an end in 1978/79. The Labour Government was pressing the issue before the 1979 elections. Faced with a likely net contribution of about £1,000 million in 1980, apparently rising fast, while Britain was still below average in income-per-head and several richer member states were net beneficaries, how could Mrs Thatcher not raise the issue?

It has also to be said that, by this time, the question had already become a test of the Community's fair dealing. The way in which France had insisted on agreement among the Six to the own-resources system before Britain could join had roused the suspicions even of British 'Europeans' that the French were trying to take financial advantage of Britain's late entry. The Heath Government's efforts to increase Community expenditure in Britain, through – for example – the Regional Fund, and the Labour 'renegotiation' had shown that the solution could not be found by increasing non-CAP expenditure and that a fair deal was going to be hard to come by. Even a less determined Prime Minister would have pressed the issue. Mrs Thatcher resolved during her first months in office that she would not rest until Britain was treated equitably.

To recapitulate, the way the Community gets its revenue is from tariffs and levies, and from VAT. The expenditure is decided by the various Councils, more than 70% going to agriculture. The level of expenditure determines what the VAT call-up will be each year – always within the ceiling.

The technical reason for the British budget problem were first, that British tariffs and levies were and are rather higher than average and higher, for example, than the British share of GNP. Britain therefore had always paid in a relatively high gross contribution. Second, and even more important, the British share of CAP expenditure has been only about 10–12% compared with a gross contribution share of 20–22%, with the result that less Community money is spent in Britain than in other member states. Britain was thus always certain to have a disproportionately large net contribution once the system was applied without the correction of the transitional period.

When this prospective problem was raised by Britain in the entry negotiations, the Community of Six did not dispute its likely existence. They said that it should disappear with time, as other Community policies developed, and argued that all that was needed was a transitional period. They had nothing specific in mind by way of expenditure then and the course of events in the late 1970s and early 1980s showed that talk about the development of other policies was only a ploy designed to head off British budget demands. But this was not yet clear at the time of the entry negotiations. So a seven-year transitional period was agreed, during which British payments into the budget rose gradually to their normal 'own resources' level. The British said that this was not enough and after difficult argument, the Community of Six finally offered the famous assurance that, if an 'unacceptable situation' were to arise, the institutions would find equitable solutions. It was on the basis of this assurance that Britain joined. The assurance was to prove useful in the 1974 'renegotiation' as evidence that the terms of entry were not complete and fair; and invaluable during the 1979–84 negotiations as an answer to those Continental critics who said that Britain had signed the Treaty and should live with the consequences.

On this issue, a real and difficult negotiation took place in 1974/75, despite the fact that we were only two years into the seven-year transitional period and it was therefore in the eyes of other member governments too early to be making a fuss. I toured the Community capitals in April 1974 with Alan Bailey of the Treasury to prepare the negotiations and was told everywhere that nothing could be done about the expenditure side; that we should have to rely on Community policies being created in new areas and expenditure going to the UK. There was just a hint that something might temporarily be done about our above-average gross contribution. And so we went for a correction on the gross contribution side.

After six months of negotiation in late 1974 and early 1975, there was some prospect that we might secure a rebate of somewhere around 100–150 million ECUs a year for the last few years of the 1970s, not large in relation to an expected net contribution of at least ten times that, but substantial all the same. But, at the Dublin European Council in March 1975, the German Finance Ministry briefed Chancellor Schmidt to propose that the operation of the corrective mechanism under discussion should be subject to conditions which, they hoped and believed, were unlikely to be fulfilled. Mr Wilson nevertheless settled on this basis.

The mechanism, with the German conditions, never produced any financial results. However, the principle was established that an inequitably large contribution to the Community budget could be corrected by a mechanism and the outcome was helpful in the referendum campaign which followed.

Throughout the 1974–75 negotiation, the other members of the Community resolutely refused to accept the validity of the concept of net contributions. Their aversion to this commonsense measure of the burden placed on a member state by the Community budget was partly due to General de Gaulle at one stage having tried to insist on the *juste retour*, i.e. that, for any given policy, no member state, at any rate not France, should pay in more than it got out. The *juste retour* in this form would indeed have been unworkable and much opprobrium was heaped on Britain in 1980–84 for allegedly demanding it. But it was nevertheless still true that the net contribution was and remains the clearest available measure of the burden borne by a member state as the result of the budget. The net beneficiaries, which in those days included France, simply did not wish the net balances even to be published. The Danes, in particular, were passionate in their opposition lest giving publicity to their net gains lead to their erosion.

After the 1975 Referendum, the budget issue lay dormant for a number of years. But it was clear that it would come back to the negotiating table at the end of the transitional period in 1979 when Britain would have to pay its full own resources contribution. So I was always looking for a chance to get the concept of net contributions accepted. That chance came in August 1978 by a great piece of luck, when the Economic Policy Committee, under the ECOFIN Council, was discussing what economic measures might be necessary in order to make it possible for the least prosperous member states to join the exchange rate mechanism of the EMS on which work was proceeding following the Bremen European Council. Italy was at that time briefly quite a substantial net contributor. So, already, was the UK. I was the Deputy Secretary in Charge of Economic Affairs in the Foreign Office, and got in touch with my old friend and opposite number in Rome, Renato Ruggiero, and together we sacrificed a few days of our August holiday, went to the Economic Policy Committee and during the course of the debate asked the Commission to produce the figures for net balances. Rather to my surprise, they agreed and, as expected, the figures showed that Britain was likely soon to overtake Germany as the major net contributor.

When Mrs Thatcher came to power in May 1979, the transitional period was ending. The net figures were on the table and showed that there was a real problem. There was a budget squeeze at home. For all the reasons given above, it was a high priority to get a fair budget settlement. Mrs Thatcher wanted a plan of campaign worked out.

The French were in the Chair that six months and, in June, the European Council was in Strasbourg. Mrs Thatcher agreed that the essential first step was to get the UK budget problem on the formal agenda of the Community. She therefore took a relatively mild approach, both with President Giscard in advance and in the meeting, and persuaded him to sum up that the Community would need to look at the problem and that the Commission should produce a factual report for discussion at the next meeting. Mrs Thatcher wrote down the words of his summing-up and gave them to me at her debriefing.

That night, the French Presidency set up a drafting group to produce draft conclusions for the Heads of Government. They tabled a draft which bore no relationship whatever to President Giscard's summing-up. It took me several hours before I was able to get the Chair to agree that the Secretary-General of the Council should read out President Giscard's summing-up. When he did so,

I said that Britain could accept the French President's wording. No one else objected.

Fortunately, there was no problem about getting the net balance figures into the Commission's report which came out in good time at the end of September. Indeed, the British budget problem came to be known as a 'problem of budget imbalances'. But when it came to getting something done to correct the situation, the going got rough. The French took the lead in laying down a restrictive line, but the other member governments broadly went along with them. The French argued that any alleviation of the British burden must be '*forfaitaire*' (i.e., a lump sum and no mechanism with objective criteria), temporary, and degressive. The British argued that, on the contrary, the solution should last as long as the problem, should be proportional to the size of the problem and should be automatic so that constant negotiation on the subject was avoided. These basic positions were maintained until nearly the end of the negotiation when most of the British arguments prevailed.

Some member governments revived the old argument that the British problem could be dealt with by the development of Community policies of net benefit to the UK. Partly in order to test this out, the British Government proposed in October 1979 (though not in the budget context) that Community energy policy, then under discussion in the light of the second big increase in the oil price of the 1970s, should include substantial Community aid for coal investment. This fitted in well with the climate of opinion which favoured reduced dependence on imported oil and would have had the added advantage of producing net benefits for Britain and Germany, the two net contributors. The Commission were helpful and Energy Ministers even agreed at an informal meeting during the Danish Presidency of 1982 that the Community should have a solid fuels policy. Britain pressed the issue regularly but a number of member governments, led by France, always blocked progress. In life you can often gain advantage from your failures as well as your successes. No one persisted in private, after about 1981, in telling us that the development of Community policies would solve the British problem. 'Now, Coal . . .' we would murmur; and the subject would be changed.

The first major clash at the political level came at the Dublin European Council in December 1979. Mrs Thatcher was determined to get progress. Chancellor Schmidt and President Giscard seemed to have agreed that they would do all they could to discourage her from pressing the issue. Mrs Thatcher would not be put off. In her Press Conference afterwards, she declared her determination 'to get our money back', a phrase which caused some genuine, and much spurious, outrage in other Community capitals. She was accused of not understanding that the Community's own resources belonged to the Community, and was told that, Britain having signed the Treaty, she had no right to demand a rebate – despite the famous declaration about the 'unacceptable situation'. And throughout the negotiation public accusations about seeking a *juste retour* went on, despite frequent British statements of willingness to remain a net contributor but on a more modest basis.

No progress had been made in Dublin. Inflation was high in many Community countries in 1980 and it was clear that the farmers would want big price increases in the spring price-fixing. Up to then, the annual CAP price-fixing had always been done by consensus, although it was a majority voting matter under the Treaty. There was a natural link between the two issues, since the CAP is the main cause of the British budget problem and a big price increase would increase our net contribution. This link was to become increasingly important as April and May passed.

In February 1980, on instructions, I tabled a proposal in COREPER for a corrective mechanism under which the UK would receive back in the following year a proportion to be decided of our net contribution. This was met with a complete refusal and the usual incantation, '*forfaitaire, temporaire, dégressif*'.

The next European Council was in Luxembourg under Italian chairmanship in April 1980. As is often done, Prime Minister Cossiga toured some of the Community capitals before the meeting and President Giscard gave him a broad hint that he wanted a settlement for two or three years at Luxembourg. Commission estimates for the UK net contribution for 1980 and 1981 were on the table at about 1800 million ECUs and 2200 million ECUs respectively.

By the second morning at Luxembourg, a real negotiation was in progress. Mrs Thatcher was reluctant to accept a settlement of less than five years, partly no doubt, in order to take the problem out of British politics until after the next election, but the others were unwilling to go beyond two. Discussion centred on this problem, on the size of the refund that Britain would get (with the highest figure for the two years which seemed perhaps to be on offer being about 2500 million ECUs) and on the question of risk-sharing if the Commission estimates proved conservative. The other Heads of Government seemed to be willing to concede an element of risk-sharing in that event. But the details remained to be settled.

There were other items to be discussed, including the Common Fisheries Policy which was at a difficult stage of negotiation. So the budget discussion was broken off for a while at about lunch-time on the second day. This did not help towards a budget solution, because the fisheries discussion became heated. The European Council never came back to a serious negotiation on the budget.

But it was already late April, and the Agriculture Council was blocked by the UK on the price-fixing. The incentive to get agreement on the budget was strong, particularly since delegations had no longer seemed to be impossibly far apart at Luxembourg.

The idea occurred to the Italian Presidency that the debate might be carried forward at the informal meeting of Foreign Ministers in Naples planned for mid-May, and Lord Carrington (then Foreign Secretary) took with him a small team including myself. All Saturday, the team sat in the sunshine on the terrace while the Foreign Ministers alone discussed other matters. They were supposed to turn to the UK budget problem on Sunday morning, and the meeting was to end with a lunch. Lord Carrington's plane was put on standby for 3.00 p.m. But Italian informal contacts overnight showed that the majority of Foreign Ministers had no stomach, perhaps no instructions, for a renewed bout of budget negotiation and so the meeting came to an abrupt and unforeseen end after breakfast. Lord Carrington's RAF crew were sought, but had disappeared to Pompeii. I remember going back towards the British Consulate in the car with Lord Carrington, who was repeating every few minutes, 'I must behave well', in a furious voice. I am happy to report that he did, even though we only managed finally to take off in the middle of the afternoon.

After consulting Lord Carrington, who said that it would be worthwhile having a special meeting of the Foreign Affairs Council, i.e. indicated a readiness to negotiate, Signor Colombo in the Chair called a special meeting of the Council for the afternoon of 29th May. It was clear from the beginning that he was determined to get a settlement. After a relatively brief formal opening of the Council, he resorted to a technique known in the Community as 'Confessionals'. He sat with Mr Roy Jenkins (President of the Commission) in the Presidency Room on the 14th Floor of the Charlemagne building and called in delegations one by one all through the evening and most of the night, gradually easing his way forward towards a compromise. The story of that night is too long to tell here. Perhaps the crucial meeting in it was one in the British Office, at which Lord Carrington and Sir Ian Gilmour did a deal at four in the morning with Herr von Dohnanyi who was representing Germany, while the French Minister, M.Bernard-Raymond, and my French colleague anxiously paced the corridor outside.

97

We emerged at about 8.00 a.m. with a three-year deal, under which Britain would get a sum corresponding to two-thirds of the Commission estimate of our net contribution for 1980 and 1981 (a total of nearly 2,600 million ECUs) with a complicated risk-sharing formula, under which Britain would get varying percentages of any excess in the net contribution over the Commission estimate. All this was accompanied by a 'Mandate' to the Commission to prepare a report on the Community's policies generally, the CAP and the problem of budget imbalances (with the 'aim to prevent the recurrence of unacceptable situations') for the European Council in 1981. If this was not achieved there was to be a solution for 1982 'along the lines of' the 1980/81 solution.

Lord Carrington, Sir Ian Gilmour, Michael Franklin, David Hannay (now my successor in Brussels) and I went home to a late breakfast, thinking that we had done a good night's work. Mrs Thatcher was at Chequers and Lord Carrington arranged to go there to explain the outcome. I gave the party a couple of bottles of champagne to celebrate in the plane.

But before they arrived at Chequers, the Prime Minister's staff were calling for detailed information, and it was clear that the Prime Minister was going to want to look at every word and comma. I remember passing a disagreeable afternoon as uncertainty joined fatigue and no news came. The telephone in my office kept ringing as my colleagues wanted to discover whether Mrs Thatcher had approved the deal, and I had to tell them 'not yet'. Thank Heaven, she did approve it before dinner.

As we saw it, the 30th May Agreement provided a breathing space during which to work for a permanent settlement, and the 30th May Mandate and the British Presidency, starting on 1st July 1981, an opportunity to get the work done. The new Thorn Commission (which came into office in January 1981) were asked to provide a report as the basis for the discussion, and did so in June 1981. A preparatory group which I chaired went to work on it in early July. Considerable progress was made on the chapter on Community policies in general, and some on the reform of the CAP where the growing surpluses were already causing deep concern. But by November, when papers had to be prepared to put to the European Council at Lancaster House in early December, there was still virtually no progress on the problem of budget imbalances. The other delegations did not yet have a real incentive to come to an agreement. One of the less sensible rules of Community life is that difficult negotiations only end in agreement a little later than the eleventh hour and fifty-ninth minute.

Mrs Thatcher did her best to push the negotiation on the 30th May Mandate forward at Lancaster House. On her instructions I chaired a drafting meeting all through the night in order to try to produce a basis for agreement among Heads of Government on the second morning. My Danish and French colleagues, however (the latter at times supported by one, sometimes two, ministers), made it impossible to submit a single draft text. Though President Mitterrand was reported not to be best pleased with the results of the night's labours, there were too many outstanding differences for it to be possible for Mrs Thatcher to lead the Council itself to an agreement. She chaired the Council with complete impartiality and did not attempt to push her colleagues beyond the points to which they were ready to go. Even if she had kept them there far into the next night, I do not think any agreement could have been reached.

The Belgians who took over on 1st January 1982 did not give a high priority to trying to complete the 30th May Mandate negotiation. Nothing therefore much happened until the spring when the price-fixing and the need to agree a figure for the 1982 refund for the UK began to come together in people's minds. But nothing was normal that spring. The Argentines invaded the Falklands in early April and the Community behaved well – and quickly. A Community arms and trade embargo was agreed within a week. But, despite the commitment on 30th May, 1980, to a solution for 1982 along the lines of 1980/81, the Germans and the French took a very tough line on the budget problem and were unwilling to offer a figure remotely near the refunds of 1180 million ECUs for 1980 and the 1410 million ECUs for 1981. (They had, it is true, the excuse that it was already clear that the outcome for 1981 was far more favourable to the UK than had been thought likely in 1980.)

Lord Carrington had resigned in early April and Mr Francis Pym nobly entered the budget fray, despite his many preoccupations over the Falklands war. Disagreeable discussions on a brilliant sunny day at a hostelry in the Ardennes, with thousands of Belgian farmers demonstrating on tractors outside, brought Foreign Ministers no further forward. A late-night meeting in Luxembourg in mid-May was equally fruitless, perhaps because by then a plot was afoot to vote the British down on the price-fixing in the Agriculture Council. Media attention to the budget battle was becoming intense. The television crews were so thick on the ground in Luxembourg that it was almost impossible for Mr Pym and his team to fight their way through to the meeting room.

As in 1980, we sought to use the pressure for CAP price-fixing decisions to bring about an agreement on the budget, planning if necessary to invoke the famous 'Luxembourg Compromise' of February 1966 to hold up the decisions on CAP prices for 1982-83. Majority voting and the veto will be dealt with in a later chapter. All that it is necessary to say here is that the 'Luxembourg Compromise' was really an agreement to differ, with the French insisting that where 'very important national interests' were at stake, discussion should continue until unanimous agreement was reached, and with the other Community governments (specially the Benelux) unequivocally opposed to the French view. To avoid a vote, enough countries must stand by the member government invoking the Luxembourg Compromise to make sure that no qualified majority can be found. The French had always stood by those invoking it and most French officials were convinced in May 1982 that President Mitterrand would continue to do so.

It is hard to say what would have happened if the Falklands War had not been at its height in mid-May. Perhaps a settlement might have been reached before the vote in the Agriculture Council. There is little doubt that the impossibility for the British of fighting two 'wars' at once was a factor in the mind of those pushing for a vote of CAP prices. We had expected that the French would stand by the Luxembourg Compromise if it was invoked. But they (and the Irish) did not, inventing a new and dubious argument that the commitment not to vote down a member state invoking it only applied where important national interests were directly (rather than indirectly) involved. As a result, when Mr Peter Walker invoked the Luxembourg Compromise in order to try to prevent a vote on the price-fixing in the Agriculture Council, only Denmark and Greece stood by the UK. Fifty or sixty votes on all the various regulations for increasing prices were taken. It was our worst defeat. The lever we had used with the success to get the 30th May settlement in 1980 was knocked from our hands. High price increases for most products, with serious consequences for the budget in 1983/84, were adopted. The French claimed that the Luxembourg Compromise was quite unimpaired; and it was not in the UK interest to argue the contrary!

With the Falkland war coming to its climax, this major setback did not become the painful crisis at Westminster which it might have done. The other member governments, perhaps feeling a little guilty, soon afterwards agreed with Mr Pym on a 1982 refund of 850 million ECUs. By this time it was known to everyone to what extent the 1981 net balance for the UK had turned out more favourably than anybody had ever expected or the Commission had forecast in May 1980. In the end, Britain only made a net contribution of 9 million ECUs in 1981, as against more than 700 million estimated under the 30th May Agreement, the other member governments having omitted during the night of 29th–30th May to ask for a risk-sharing formula downwards to match the risk-sharing upwards on which we had insisted. This fact, and the difficulty of fighting a major battle in Europe as well as the Falklands War, pushed Britain towards accepting a lower figure for 1982 than for 1980 or 1981.

Both sides thought it better to let the budget problem rest for a while after these exertions. Britain had no need to push it forward in the immediate future. Lacking the 1980 lever of the linkage with the price-fixing, we were looking for a new instrument to help us to achieve a satisfactory long-term settlement. By good fortune, one was to hand which could not legally be circumvented. It was already clear in late 1982, especially since the 1982 price rises had triggered a very big increase in the cost of the CAP, that the money within the 1% VAT ceiling was going to be exhausted within a year or so. The 1% ceiling could only be raised by unanimous agreement between the national governments and after ratification by their national Parliaments. Officials recommended to British ministers that we should try during 1983 to set up a major Community negotiation covering the possibility of an increase in the 1% ceiling, the reform of the CAP, the need for budget discipline (and in particular for a binding guideline that the rate of growth of CAP expenditure should not exceed the rate of growth of the Own Resources base) and, of course, the eternal problem of budget imbalances.

Mrs Thatcher did not commit herself to this scenario untl the early hours of the first night of the Stuttgart European Council in June 1983, though she had indicated beforehand that she recognised the arguments in favour of a negotiation of this kind. The instructions she gave in the small hours for the drafting of a statement in the Council on the subject the next day were to make it 100% clear that she would only agree to consider an increase in own resources if all her conditions about budget imbalances and budget discipline were met.

The Stuttgart meeting again spent a lot of time on the British budget problem because Mrs Thatcher had to insist that it should fix our 1983 refund as well as setting up the long-term negotiation, since the figure needed to go into the 1984 budget which was then under negotiation. The French were reluctant to offer anything and certainly not a sum which Mrs Thatcher could regard as being in her area of negotiation.

Chancellor Kohl, who was in the Chair, showed great determination. I remember vividly one of the pauses in the discussion. Half an hour of private meetings in small groups had got nowhere. President Mitterand and Chancellor Kohl were in animated argument through an interpreter. The French were giving it out that President Mitterrand was about to leave and, indeed, at one moment he moved towards the door, only to be brought back by Chancellor Kohl. Fortunately, the Germans had foreseen a long negotiation and had got agreement that Stuttgart should, as an exception, go into a third day. President Mitterrand did leave on the second evening and M. Mauroy took his place. But eventually full agreement was reached on the Declaration in a form entirely satisfactory to Britain since it made clear that all the issues were to be settled together, i.e. no increase in Own Resources without agreement on budget discipline and a settlement on budget imbalances. There was also in the end a settlement on the UK 1983 refund at 750 million ECUs. Mrs Thatcher decided to accept this relatively low sum on the basis that, if the UK refunds for the four years 1980–83 were added together, the total would come to approximately two-thirds of the UK net contribution for those years (because of our low net contribution in 1981 and the 'overpayment' to the UK in that year).

It is worth recounting in this connection a small example of the sharpness of Community negotiating techniques. During the discussions in the autumn of 1982 about the inclusion of the 1982 refund in the 1983 draft budget, the French and the Danes had advanced the intrinsically absurd proposition that the 850 million ECUs refund for 1982 should not be net, i.e. that the British should contribute their normal budget share of 20% or so towards their own refund. This demand was probably only put forward as a negotiating ploy and was eventually dropped. But the brief for Stuttgart brought out the need to avoid any repetition of this tiresome argument in 1983. So Mrs Thatcher insisted in the Council that the short text tabled on the UK refund for 1983 should contain the word 'net' after the figure of 750 million ECUs, and this was agreed. Behind the scenes we were able, after a short argument, to persuade the German Presidency that this text ought to be published alongside the main Stuttgart Declaration.

While Mrs Thatcher was debriefing to the delegation at the end of the meeting, the final version of the four-line budget text, together with the text of the Stuttgart Declaration, were brought up from the Council Secretariat and I noticed that the word 'net' had been left out. I excused myself and literally ran to the Presidency Office because these texts were about to be distributed to the press. I found a German Foreign Ministry official and asked him to insert the word 'net' in a revised version, as agreed in the Council. He prevaricated. I insisted that Mrs Thatcher had secured the Council's agreement to its inclusion. After a moment's pause, he and my German colleague, who now appeared, agreed. A revised four-line text was typed and I carried it back to the British Delegation room.

In a long Community negotiation, ministers and officials can never afford to relax. A moment's inattention during the summing-up by the President of the

Council can, for example, lose you much of the ground gained during a whole day of discussion. Progress is made slowly, step by step, month by month, word by word. You have to make quite sure that you never allow a procedural move or the wording of a conclusion of a Council to lose you an inch of the ground gained.

It is clear in retrospect that the Stuttgart Declaration was the watershed in the whole five-year negotiation. Other members of the Community now had just as strong an incentive as the UK to want the post-Stuttgart negotiation to succeed. Another crucial point was that to increase the 1% VAT ceiling, the 1970 own resources decision had to be amended, with all ten parliaments ratifying the amendments. If the solution to the UK budget problem were incorporated in a revised own resources decision, it would be a decisive advance. Mrs Thatcher clearly recognized the significance of Stuttgart and gave a small party at No. 10 Downing St the following week for all those who had played a part in preparing the meeting or advising her during it.

The Greeks took over the Chair from the Germans in July and work started in accordance with the Stuttgart Declaration. All that autumn an endless series of preparatory groups and special Councils of Foreign, Finance and Agriculture Ministers, both under the chairmanship of the unfortunate Mr Varfis, the Greek Deputy Minister (and since 1985 Commissioner) took place in Athens and Brussels. Sir Geoffrey Howe plugged away relentlessly in favour of an automatic solution to the problem of budget imbalances which would last as long as the problem and be put into effect through the new own resources decision by a deduction of VAT in the following year. The old cries of *'forfaitaire, temporaire, dégressif'* were more muted now, but not stilled. Miraculously Sir Geoffrey Howe managed to make a good little joke here or a new point there and to keep his colleagues in good humour without ever giving ground.

No European Council has ever been so long prepared as the Athens European Council and quite a lot of good work was in fact done. But the European Council itself spent the whole of the first day on Agriculture, including the vexed question of milk quotas. Moreover, when the Council turned to the question of budget imbalances, the French took a line which went back on the progress already made. Many observers thought that they wished to make sure that the post-Stuttgart negotiation ended not in Athens but at one of the European Councils in the French Presidency which was about to begin. If so, they were entirely succesful. Nothing of any kind was agreed in Athens.

It is hard to be sure, but President Mitterand had probably decided after

Stuttgart that the British budget problem had got to be settled. More Community money was needed if the CAP was to continue to be financed at a level which was politically tolerable in France. With Spanish and Portuguese accession now something which President Mitterand felt had to be accepted, France was clearly about to become an important net contributor. A concession to Britain by France on the budget could probably be wrapped up in a major package which could be made the triumphant outcome of the French Presidency. At all events the atmosphere changed early in 1984 and France and Britain started to work together in a way which they had not done before.

They remained in very close touch throughout the French Presidency. Sir Geoffrey Howe had frequent and fruitful bilateral meetings with M. Dumas, then Minister for European Affairs. Gradually the basis for a settlement began to be established. It became, for example, common ground that the UK refunds should in future take the form of a deduction of VAT in the following year; and that, to this end, the budget imbalance arrangement should be an integral part of the new own resources decision which would be required if the 1% ceiling were to be raised. This was an important concession on the French side, since it implied that the arrangement would last for as long as the new own resources decision lasted, and would be automatic. It also had the major advantage that it would make it much more difficult for the European Parliament to cause trouble over the refunds which they had been doing increasingly in the two previous years when the money had had to be put through the expenditure side of the budget.

The French arranged virtually no multilateral discussion before their first European Council in Brussels in March. They played their cards close to their chests and nobody was sure whether they wished to make serious progress in March or whether, as they hinted once or twice, they were proposing to bring the whole complex of questions to a settlement after their municipal elections in May at the Fontainebleau European Council.

Throughout the autumn of 1983 and in early 1984, the concept of net contributions had been causing renewed trouble. The French and most other member states were now arguing the opposite of what they had argued in 1974, namely that any corrective mechanism could only take account of the lack of Community expenditure in the UK and not of Britain's above-average gross contribution. It was argued, not only that the very concept of net contributions was pernicious and smacked of the *juste retour* (whether or not the refund was only a percentage of the net contribution), which was clearly not the case, but also that the tariffs and levies were in some mystical way even more the property of the Community than the VAT call-up under the own resources decision and that no correction should be provided in regard to British payments of tariffs and levies.

I remember discussing this problem with Hans Tietmeyer (State Secretary in the German Finance Ministry) one evening at dinner in the autumn of 1983 at the British Embassy in Luxembourg. It was clear to us both that agreement would be impossible unless some unambiguous way of measuring the size of the budget imbalance, a proportion of which was to be corrected, could be found. We talked about various alternatives which had been put forward, such as using the difference between the British expenditure share and its GNP share – or even its population share – of the budget. But the only one which, it seemed to me, might just possibly be acceptable to Mrs Thatcher, was to use the difference between the British share of Community expenditure and the British share of VAT payments. This had the serious disadvantage that it understated the British net contribution by 200-300 million ECUs (out of a total of, say, 2,000 million ECUs at the time). But the tariffs and levies were in any case declining as a percentage of the gross contribution and there were some reasons for thinking that the British contribution of tariffs and levies would gradually come nearer its VAT share. Furthermore, the idea had three major advantages:

> First, at the margin, the VAT share/expenditure share gap was the same as our net contribution, so that any *increase* in our net contribution would be fully covered;
> Second, it did not leave the tariffs and levies out of the account but only scaled them down to the VAT share; and
> Third, it might provide an acceptable compromise to save the face of the other member states who were arguing that the tariffs and levies should be left out of the account altogether.

Shortly afterwards, the Germans officially proposed the use of the VAT share/expenditure share gap as a measure of what was to be corrected, and the idea gradually gained supporters among those involved in the negotiation. By the time of the Brussels European Council at the end of March 1984, it seemed certain to get accepted in the end and Mrs Thatcher decided to make the concession in her speech on the first day as a sign of a desire to settle.

It is not perhaps surprising that few of the Heads of Government, to whom the problem was of less consuming interest than it was for us, found it easy to understand the nature of VAT share/expenditure share gap! At any rate, several of them continued, at the afternoon session, to play the old record about tariffs and levies being completely different and having to be left out of account. Mrs Thatcher decided that the issue had got to be cleared up and argued vigorously over dinner, complete with her Treaty in her handbag, that there was no intrinsic difference between VAT and tariffs and levies. Other Heads of Government reacted on stock lines and some hours of heated argument took place. To the British team, waiting for Mrs Thatcher to return, reports of this argument began to filter through at about 10.00 p.m. and seemed difficult to explain since our information from all the other delegations was that they were prepared to accept the VAT share/expenditure share gap.

When Mrs Thatcher returned to my house well after midnight, she considered with Sir Geoffrey Howe, David Williamson of the Cabinet Office, and myself what she should do next. The situation was less promising than we had hoped. Not only had the argument at dinner been unnecessary, but the French Presidency had so far failed to table a proposal reflecting the long talks Sir Geoffrey Howe had had with M. Dumas. Mrs Thatcher decided to see President Mitterrand first thing in the morning, to indicate a readiness to negotiate along the lines already discussed with the French by the Foreign Secretary and to try to get him to instruct his team to agree a paper on a corrective mechanism with us.

We were up early and prepared a speaking note for use with President Mitterrand, who agreed to see her at the Charlemagne building before the European Council. The Foreign Ministers were meeting to discuss something else at that time and so she took me with her. The meeting went well and President Mitterrand said that he would send someone to our office very shortly. Mrs Thatcher said I would be waiting for them.

M. Dumas arrived with Guy Legras of the Quai d'Orsay and, in half an hour, together with David Williamson and David Hannay (then the under-Secretary in Charge of the Community in the Foreign Office, and now my successor in Brussels), we negotiated a satisfactory text which, after some delay, the French Presidency tabled before lunch. (The mechanism involved was pretty complicated and I do not propose to describe it in detail because it was superseded at Fontainebleau in June). One of the last problems outstanding was the duration of the correcting mechanism and that was settled by saying that it would be part of the new own resources decision 'their durations being linked', a formula which Hannay and Legras had tentatively agreed the night before. So the French could say there was a limited duration and the British could say that the mechanism will continue until there is British agreement to change it! In substance, the British had what they wanted. This wording was retained in June.

This agreement was an enormous step forward since the paper contained all the elements we required, except the figures which would be needed in order to make it operational and which Heads of Government were supposed to negotiate in the Council. Unfortunately, the discussion there went less well because the German delegation made a sudden proposal in the European Council for a flat-rate refund of 1,000 million ECUs for a number of years. This was completely unacceptable to Britain. One or two other Heads of Government saw problems about accepting the mechanism in the Presidency paper on the spot. The French, with support from others, tried to set the opening figure well below our minimum requirements, at 1,000 million ECUs in the first year of the new system. This was unacceptable to Mrs Thatcher since it would only have given a refund percentage of only 50% or a little more. She made a final effort and proposed that there should be one last year of *ad hoc* refunds for 1984 at 1,000 million ECUs and that the new system should start on the basis of 1,300 million in regard to 1985. But this was not accepted by the others. So the meeting had to adjourn without a conclusion.

Following the March European Council, with the negotiation blocked on the difference between 1,000 million ECUs as the 'guide' figure which the other nine member states were prepared to offer and the higher figure we required, no progress was made in three further rounds of discussion in the Foreign Ministers' Council in Brussels. To overcome this impasse while securing exactly the same results from our point of view, it was necessary to find a way of changing somewhat the angle of approach. This was done through some quiet diplomacy with the French in the run up to the Fontainebleau meeting. From contacts between Sir Geoffrey Howe and M. Dumas and their officials we got the impression that the French wanted to get a settlement at Fontainebleau in June, if possible, and would rather prefer to get away from the complicated mechanism in the Presidency paper tabled at Brussels; and that an alternative approach which might be accepted by them was to limit the application of the mechanism to the UK only and to base the correction of our contribution on a rebate to the United Kingdom in the following year of a simple percentage of our VAT share/expenditure share gap.

Despite the progress made in these contacts, on the day before the meeting it was still not entirely clear how President Mitterrand planned to handle it. Just before the Prime Minister set off for Fontainebleau, a completely different and unacceptable French proposal was circulated which had to be rejected.

There was a brief discussion in the European Council on the first afternoon, though the French were letting it be known that a revised Presidency Paper would appear the next morning. That evening, M. Dumas and Guy Legras were friendly but elusive. Heads of Government had dinner in a charming inn in the forest and two or three British officials and President Mitterrand's own closest advisers from the Elysée, Bianco and Attali, sat in the courtyard waiting to find out if anything had happened. We chatted amicably, but they had nothing interesting to say on the budget question. In the end the Heads of Government hardly touched on it over dinner. So the negotiation seemed to be hanging fire.

Around midnight, M. Dumas gave the go-ahead for us to discuss a revised draft paper on the lines we had expected with Guy Legras. But he was staying in another hotel some kilometres away, and the British delegation in a third. Robin Renwick (who had taken over from David Hannay) discussed the paper with Legras on the telephone and agreed that they and David Williamson should meet very early in the morning. Meanwhile, I reported to Mrs Thatcher at breakfast time in her hotel.

When we got to the Château, there was one point in the new paper negotiated with the French which was still causing problems. At Brussels we had agreed with the French on a text which would have made it clear that any increase in our net contribution due to the entry of Spain and Portugal in 1986 would be subject to the corrective mechanism in the normal way. The French were now trying to get in a paragraph which said the opposite. I objected strongly. Legras saw our point but had no flexibility in his instructions. Apart from this point, the only thing that was missing – and this a large one – if a satisfactory solution was to be achieved was the percentage refund of our VAT share/expenditure share gap. The Prime Minister had instructed us to talk about something over 70% (to compensate for using the VAT share/ expenditure share gap instead of the net contribution). The French and others were talking about 50–55%.

Meanwhile, the German Finance Ministry were not content. Nothing was being done for Germany, whereas in 1982 and 1983, the Germans had insisted successfully on being let off half their contribution to British refunds. A rugger scrum of Germans round the massive figure of Chancellor Kohl seemed to be becoming excited. This was worrying, remembering what had happened in Brussels.

The European Council met on time, but did not continue in formal session for long. Mrs Thatcher and her colleagues were still some way apart on the percentage. President Mitterrand called a pause for 'bilaterals'.

Mrs Thatcher's bilateral with Chancellor Kohl showed that he would insist on getting a refund for Germany of a part of the normal German contribution to the British refund. Luckily no one seemed to be disposed to disagree with him.

As for the percentage, he was firmly stuck at a maximum of 60%. In Mrs Thatcher's bilateral with President Mitterrand, he indicated that he might just be prepared to go to 65% in order to settle. Meanwhile, we were hearing from other delegations that 60% or just possibly 65% was the limit and that there was no question of anything like 70%. As the minutes passed it began to seem certain that 65% was negotiable.

There were a number of corridors and small rooms off the main meeting-room and Mrs Thatcher told Sir Geoffrey Howe, David Williamson and myself that she wanted a private word with us in one of them. On the way there, David Williamson, a born negotiator and an old Community hand, said to me: 'The time has come to settle this negotiation now. We must advise her to settle.' I said: 'Yes, but don't rush in, let's see what she says.' The four of us sat in a little room and there was quite a long silence while Mrs Thatcher thought. Then she turned to us and said: 'It's time to settle'. She had come to the same conclusion.

She saw President Mitterrand and indicated a desire to settle, but said that it would be helpful to her to have 66% rather than 65% (the 30th May Agreement had been two-thirds of the net contribution and each 1% was likely to be worth about £15 million a year). He suggested she raise this in the meeting. She did, and got her way.

Meanwhile, the French tabled the paper we had almost agreed with them, but with the offending paragraph about enlargement in it. We rightly suspected that this would cost us a lot of money if accepted. Mrs Thatcher argued strongly against it and got her way. The paper was then approved.

Thus the great budget negotiation ended with our getting agreement that the new own resources decision should include one more year of *ad hoc* refund at 1,000 million ECUs for 1984 and after that a deduction from the British VAT payment in the following year of 66% of the British VAT share/expenditure share gap – an outcome very close indeed to what we had been trying for in February 1980.

To keep this story from becoming intolerably long, I have not dealt step-by-step with the other elements in the post-Stuttgart package. It is enough to say here that the Agriculture Council reached agreement in March 1984 on milk quotas and on a commitment to apply 'guarantee thresholds' to other products in surplus, and that the ECOFIN Council, after some delay, finally agreed a conclusion on budget discipline in the autumn of 1984 which contained a firm statement that the rate of growth of CAP expenditure shall in future be below the rate of growth of the own resources base. So the conditions that Mrs Thatcher had laid down at Stuttgart for agreeing to raise the 1% ceiling to 1.4% were fulfilled.

Work on drafting the new own resources decision which incorporates the Fontainebleau corrective mechanism was protracted and not without controversy. As is often the case in the Community, not all the differences were settled in Fontainebleau. But as far as the UK budget problem was concerned, the only serious remaining difficulty was to get the wording of the new own resources decision agreed and sent to national Parliaments in time for it to be ratified before the end of 1985.

Because of the rebate, the British VAT contribution will not go above 1% as long as the ceiling for the others is at 1.4% (and would scarcely do so even at 1.6%). So the final package contained some progress on budget discipline and the beginning of agricultural reform as well as a budget mechanism for the UK in return for allowing other member states to increase their contribution!

The Fontainebleau mechanism in its present form may not last for ever. Before long, there will be strong pressure to raise the 1.4% ceiling. The Fontainebleau conclusions themselves indicated, without commitment, that it might be raised to 1.6% in 1988. But it is not true, as some people have alleged, that the mechanism is temporary or precarious. To raise the VAT ceiling again would mean, if it were to be agreed, changing the own resources decision yet again. Clearly no British Government is going to agree to raise the 1.4% ceiling unless the British budget problem continues to be dealt with at least as satisfactorily as at Fontainebleau, if not better. Unless a new own resources decision to raise the ceiling again is agreed, the Fontainebleau mechanism will continue to be the law of the Community.

Our uncorrected net contribution has been rising fast and will rise further as a result of enlargement. In consequence, as a result of the first year of the operation of the new system in 1985, well over £1,000 million will be deducted from our 1986 VAT payments into the Community, 66% of our VAT share/expenditure share gap in 1985.

The Prime Minister, three Foreign Secretaries, two Chancellors of the Exchequer, and a slowly changing team of officials carried the 1979–84 budget campaign through to a successful conclusion. All played important parts at different times. But Mrs Thatcher herself bore the brunt of the worst moments. She herself had to negotiate points of great difficulty at Strasbourg, Dublin, Luxembourg, Stuttgart, Athens, Brussels, and Fontainebleau. She always devoted the necessary time to understanding the complications. She was inflexible in her determination to get a fair deal, but flexible on the lesser points of substance when she needed to be. If the going got rough at times, it was because very large amounts of money were at stake and others were slow to settle on a fair basis. The negotiation demonstrated that you can only get your

110

way in the Community by sustained will-power, careful planning and skilled negotiation; but also that, if you have these things and a good case, the Community has in the end to take account of it. The British had a good case.

As a postscript, there is one point to be remembered for future negotiations, when the Germans and French may want some mechanism to limit their own contributions in the next own resources decision. While in the case of the UK the VAT share/expenditure share gap is slightly smaller than the real gap (the net contribution), it is quite a lot bigger in the case of Germany and France. There is no reason why they should be allowed to make a windfall gain by using it as the basis for any correction applying to them. But I do not suppose that they will easily be persuaded to use the net contribution as the measure of the gap to be corrected!

8

Britain in Europe

BRITISH POLICY is in constitutional theory always laid down by ministers. In practice, of course, a weak or idle minister can simply rubber-stamp the recommendations of officials, in which case the reality is that the policy is decided by officials. No one is accusing Mrs Thatcher or Sir Geoffrey Howe of being weak or idle. Especially on anything to do with the European Community, which is always the subject of political controversy at home, ministers take a close interest and all the strategic decisions and many of the tactical ones are theirs.

To say this is not to deny that officials often play an important part in the policy-making process; and their role may be greater in Community than in purely home affairs. At home ministers need to know the facts and to have the best analysis that can be made of the pros and cons, including the estimated cost, of the various options under consideration. Thus armed, they are the people who know best what option fits in with their overall policies and what the impact will be on home politics.

Ministers need the same sort of analysis on questions for decision in the Community, but in addition there are new dimensions. First, on any individual subject, good policy decisions in the Community must be based on a sound estimate of the views and aims of the Commission and other member governments. Ways have to be found of reconciling national interests and government policies with those of other countries. It is no good having a perfect line from the point of view of British interests or politics if there is no hope of getting our way on that basis in the Community. In practice, it is often relatively easy to reconcile conflicting views in Brussels if an accurate assessment has been made of what others are likely to want and imaginative solutions are thought up which meet the needs of all who have a major interest. Very few Community negotiations are zero sum games in which there must always be an equivalent loss to offset a gain. Usually almost everyone can gain something.

Secondly, to quite an important extent, Community policy has to be seen as a whole and each individual policy related to it. It is only too easy to take a line on one subject which is inconsistent with what the Government is trying to do on another, possibly more important, subject. This almost always proves fatal in the Council. Officials from the Permanent Representation, the Cabinet Office and the Foreign Office who deal with a wide range of Community business and are skilled at getting their way in the Council need to join the Minister responsible and his own officials in formulating objectives, strategy and tactics.

Teamwork is therefore essential. At senior official level the Permanent Representative and his staff need to form an integral part of the Whitehall team which works on the policy papers for ministers. And ministers and officials need to work as a team in Brussels in order to get their way. What is in the end decided in the Council will depend to an important degree on preparatory contacts with the Commission and the work of COREPER and Working Groups.

It is often hard to disentangle the policy from the politics (the French only have one word for the two things). Speaking in COREPER or the Council and briefing members of the European Parliament and the British and foreign press, day in and day out, the Permanent Representative has not only to think how best to put the case in order to get things done in Brussels, but also to bear in mind the home audience and the possibility that his ministers will have to answer questions about what he has been doing or saying in the House of Commons.

Life would rapidly become hard to bear if the government adopted policies which he could not advocate sincerely. It would be extremely difficult to sustain, week in and week out, in COREPER and private conversation with colleagues, in negotiation with the Commission and in briefing the press, any line of policy which one believed to be flawed. Yet if these people think that a Permanent Representative does not really believe in his government's case, they will not bestir themselves to take account of it. To be effective he needs to feel a full member of the team.

I found no difficulty in this respect during my six years in Brussels. Of course, I also had to spend quite a lot of time explaining the views of other members of the Community in London! To do that is not, as Mr Tony Benn suggested in a 'No, Minister' programme in which we both took part, to put oneself in the position of changing loyalties or putting Europe above the national interest. It is a necessary and proper role for the Permanent Representative to play if he is to help the government to get its way.

The most politically difficult Community problems are often complicated and technical, for example, the level of car exhaust emissions consistent with the likely state of lean-burn technology over the next few years, or whether to approve the beginning of a Community programme of research into broad-band telecommunications technology. (As before, I quote real examples without explaining them, because each subject would merit a chapter, or even a book, if it were to be explained properly.) When officials see that a negotiation on such subjects is beginning in Brussels, they always try to prepare papers for ministers in good time so that instructions can be given to the Permanent Representative and his staff for the early stages during which they can often push the discussion in the direction the government wants.

Furthermore, outside interest groups want to know what the government is doing, the Press and Parliament ask questions, and the other governments in the Community seek our views. British ambassadors in Community posts need to be ready to put them across. So ministers need to consider early on where British interests lie, what other member states are likely to want, and what would be an acceptable outcome of the negotiation. The government's policy, as it is stated publicly at the beginning, needs to be consistent with its negotiating line throughout – and preferably with the outcome. It is quite difficult to change a position, once it has been stated publicly, to take account of the views of other members of the Community. There will always be a lobby determined to stop it being changed.

For all these reasons, and above all because the British team needs to know at each crucial stage of any long drawn-out, important negotiation that the Prime Minister and her colleagues are happy with what is being done, forward planning is essential. In a negotiation which is done at various levels (Working Group, COREPER, Council, European Council) those who are most likely to get their way are those who speak with one voice. But naturally it is essential not to make all the concessions in the government's negotiating position at a level below the top or prematurely at that level. Ministers need to have something to contribute to the give-and-take of the last hours of the negotiation.

The Permanent Representative and his staff therefore have an input to make into decision-making at home. The staff are in permanent contact by correspondence and telephone and often attend working meetings in London.

It is well-established practice that the Permanent Representative should work in London at least one day a week.

Early each week, the Cabinet Office, the Foreign Office, and the Permanent Representative and his staff consider what are the questions on which decisions are going to be called for in Brussels in forthcoming Councils and whether Ministers have laid down a sufficient line of policy for the time being. Where a new major issue seems likely to arise or where some change in existing policy seems likely to become necessary if we are to get our way in the Council, an item is put on the agenda of the Permanent Representative's Friday meeting with the Whitehall official team – a team which varies for each subject, but on which all the interested home departments are naturally represented. The team all know each other well and much more often than not are able to reach agreement either on tactics within existing policy laid down by ministers, or on recommendations to ministers. If policy has not yet been decided or if officials cannot agree on tactics, the issues and options are set out in papers for ministers to consider.

As a result of the meeting each week, action of various kinds gets taken. Papers are written for ministers; briefs for Council meetings are prepared; instructions are sent to British ambassadors in Community posts to speak to their governments; the UK representation in Brussels is told to speak to the Commission. But from my own point of view, almost the most important consequence of all these journeys to London was that I knew exactly what ministers and officials in London were thinking. Every day in Brussels new issues arose or old ones changed. The Permanent Representative needs to be prepared to respond when matters come up in COREPER or meetings with the Commission or other governments and to take the initiative in trying to move things in the right direction.

On Fridays, in addition to my meetings in the Cabinet Office, I would every month or two attend one of the Foreign Secretary's meetings in preparation for a Council. And quite often on another day in the week, I would have to fit in a visit to London to attend a meeting with Sir Geoffrey Howe or Mrs Thatcher herself.

Meetings at 10 Downing Street will be among my most vivid memories of all the events of these six crowded years. No meeting Mrs Thatcher chairs is ever dull. On the European Community, at any rate, there are normally vigorous exchanges of arguments. Mrs Thatcher, though thoroughly convinced of the need to make the Community work properly, is – to say the least – not automatically in favour of Commission proposals which involve sharing more sovereignty or spending the tax-payers' money through the Community budget! It is often a Permanent Representative's duty to argue in favour of one or other of these things. He needs to have a good case.

Meetings with Mrs Thatcher are not for the faint-hearted or the ill-briefed. She has normally read all the papers on the subjects under discussion, probably in the middle of the night when her ministers and advisers sleep. She will frequently launch a ferocious attack on a possible weak point in the arguments she is advised to accept. She expects her ministers and officials to defend them with equal vigour if they believe they are right. She will interrupt them if they say something she disagrees with – and yet listen intently if they insist and prove to have an important point to make which she needs to consider. It sometimes seemed to me that she would on occasion tease her advisers by advancing some outrageous proposition in which she did not believe, just to see how they responded to it.

Contrary to what is generally written in the newspapers and believed by her critics, she seemed to me positively to welcome serious argument and to have a high regard for those who argued with her most effectively. She likes a tough exchange, as I have several times heard her explain to Heads of Government from other Community countries whom she has treated to a frank expression of her views. 'That', she says, to their astonishment after a brisk exchange in the European Council, 'is how we reach decisions at home.' And this is true, though her ministers and officials do not always know at the time of their discussion with her whether their recommendations have been accepted. Just occasionally, I have heard her say 'you are doing quite well', after a particularly difficult corner in the discussion has been turned. But more often it is not clear until later, until – let us say – she is going through her speaking notes, frequently already revised on her instructions, in the plane on the way to the meeting, how far she has accepted the advice she has been offered.

AS OTHERS SEE US

Community negotiations often have a strong propaganda element, the British budget negotiation perhaps more than any other. The other member states engaged in a barrage of propaganda designed to present their defence of their own interests in a good light, to strengthen their common front and to sap British determination to carry on until a fair deal was obtained. Britain was accused of excessive nationalism, of not being interested in the Community making progress, even of blocking it, and of only being interested in money. The pro-European opponents of the government at home picked up these themes and played them back to the Continental press. Those who made such accusations no doubt believed them to be at least partly true. But it also suited them to have them highlighted. It helped to keep the resistance of the others to 'giving in' to the British more solid. As a result, the great budget negotiation played an important part in confirming the public opinion in other member states in the view that Britain was not a good member.

But Britain's poor reputation in Europe dates back to the late nineteen fifties. The British, having stood aside from the Messina Conference and thus not having been in on the drafting of the Treaty of Rome, rapidly woke up to the fact that it was going to be against British interests for there to be a united Europe of which Britain was not a member. Their response was the creation of the European Free Trade Area (EFTA) with the Scandinavians, Austria, Switzerland and Portugal. To the extent that this was conceived of as a counter to the Community, it was ineffective. But it was the origin of the myth, believed in by many French people to this day, that the British do not want a united Europe, only a free trade area. It is an odd accusation to make in the mid-eighties when the Community is already miles beyond a free trade area and the British are among the strongest advocates of rapid movement to complete the internal market which will involve a substantial addition to the area of shared sovereignty.

This is not the place to describe the course of the first entry negotiations in 1961–63. It is enough to say that, in my view, General de Gaulle's veto of British membership in January 1963 was based on his private belief that Britain would be too 'Communautaire' (perhaps best translated Community-minded) as a player of the Community game, not the opposite. He was profoundly opposed to the Jean Monnet thesis about European integration, and was still in those days hoping at least to empty the Community of its supra-national content, if not to replace it by a 'political union' which would in practice have been no more than a classical treaty for co-operation between governments and a way of asserting French leadership in Europe. (His views about treaties are on record, in relation to the Franco-German Treaty of 1963, 'They [treaties] are like young girls and roses. They last as long as they last.' He made this remark only a month or two after it was signed when fed up with the Germans for not following his line.) He believed that the Americans were trying to use European integration to dominate Europe; that he was going to have a great fight in his remaining years to try to wean Germany, in particular, away from them; and that if Britain joined, the pro-integration, pro-American front would be strengthened. But the old man was a master of political propaganda and he justified the veto by claiming that Britain was not European enough.

The veto aroused great passions on the Continent, as did General de Gaulle's subsequent campaign in 1965 against majority voting, when France left an empty chair for seven months. In my view, by an odd quirk of history, both these things came together in the early 1970s to cast a shadow over Britain's reputation in 'European' circles. General de Gaulle's propaganda campaign against Britain's European aspirations in 1963 left quite an important residue in the minds not only of Frenchmen but of others. Mr Heath's strong espousal of the veto in his political campaign to take Britain into the Community in 1971–72, during which he made the Luxembourg Compromise sound a more formal veto right than it is, made the 'Europeans' think of Britain as Gaullist which in their minds was to be anti-Community. People like the Dutch, who had had exaggerated hopes of Britain changing things for the better in the early 1960s, were beginning to be disappointed before Britain had even joined.

In the entry negotiations of 1970–71, the French drove a hard bargain, with the results on the budget which we have just examined. They also rammed through the Council a Common Fisheries Policy clearly not in Britain's interests, just before the negotiations were completed. This was a major factor in the Norwegian Government losing its referendum on membership in 1972, and was to cause Britain great difficulties later when, in the mid 1970s, the move to 200-mile limits took place.

The first half of the negotiations for a revised Common Fisheries' Policy (1976-79) darkened Britain's reputation further in the eyes of the other member governments. Mr Silkin's use of the veto convinced the others that he was not genuinely trying to achieve a negotiated settlement, with the result that many of them nursed a grievance. Mr Benn caused similar umbrage by other means in the Energy Council.

The stiff entry terms and the Labour Party's rejection of them, the anti-Market campaign by the left wing of the Labour Party and by the right wing of the Conservative Party, the so-called renegotiation of 1974–75, produced over the years thousands of headlines in Continental newspapers suggesting that Britain was a difficult and recalcitrant member. It is remarkable to what an extent people draw their view of the world from the series of headlines that their eyes catch, even if they don't read the whole article.

Another factor was that the 1973 oil crisis and the great inflation of the mid-seventies, combined with the political effects of national budget stringency which had become necessary in all member states, had made life in the Community less easy. This not only made Britain's adjustment to the Community more difficult, but created a widespread belief in the other member states that the Community of Six had been a Golden Age. People seem easily to forget that the battles between General de Gaulle and the other five were far more passionate and the philosophical divisions far deeper than those between the UK and the rest over the British budget problem in 1979–84.

The cumulative effect of all this was that, when Mrs Thatcher's government came to power in 1979 with a fundamentally pro-Community policy and engaged in the campaign for a fair deal on the budget, people in the other member states were predisposed to believe that the British were bad Europeans. Some of her language, such as 'our money', at Dublin, genuinely shocked pro-Community people. And of course no one likes losing a long-drawn-out battle, especially if it costs you a great deal of money. Fontainebleau will cost the others collectively more than £1,000 million a year for the foreseeable future. In such circumstances, minor sins of nationalistic behaviour by Britain which would probably pass unnoticed and certainly unreproached if committed by France, lead to new headlines in which Britain appears in a bad light.

Objectively, the charge that the British have been bad Europeans in recent years is hard to sustain. The other member governments grudgingly recognised that we had a case on the budget and after five years agreed something very like what we were asking at the beginning. If the campaign had to go on for five years, it was because they were slow to grasp the nettle. And at the end of the campaign, we still remain the second largest net contributor to the Community budget after Germany, though soon to be overtaken by France, while all the other member states remained net beneficiaries. So much for the *juste retour*!

Nor did Britain prove difficult or unco-operative on other things. Contrary to a French myth, now perhaps partly dissipated, Britain never tried, even under the Labour Government, to destroy the CAP, but only to get agreement that the essential steps to reform it in its own interest should be taken. We accepted a Common Fisheries Policy to which British waters contribute 60% of the fish. We have been pushing actively for full implementation of the Treaty of Rome and the completion of the single internal market. We have not vetoed the pet projects of others, even such expensive things as the Integrated Mediterranean Programmes. We have a better record of compliance with the Treaty and the judgements of the Court than most of the founder members, especially France and Italy. We have consistently argued for Community solidarity and common positions in international affairs. It is not true that we are more prone to pursue our national interests than others. All member governments do so, though some of them are more skilled than we are at concealing the fact.

The 1985 debate about majority voting and the powers of the Parliament (see

119

Chapter Twelve) has been a recent, though minor, contributory factor. The majority vote in favour of an inter-governmental conference to revise the Treaty at the Milan European Council in June 1985 produced another crop of the old headlines. But this was essentially a procedural and ephemeral issue. Milan in June was followed by Luxembourg in December, when Mrs Thatcher played a role which was generally thought to be very constructive. On the substance of the constitutional questions the British position has not been far from that of France; and the differences between Britain and Germany were marginal. There are no governments now arguing for major early steps towards federation.

But the debate about constitutional issues has brought to the surface another cause for our continuing to some extent to appear to be the odd man out, though of course not nearly so much as Denmark. Because of public attitudes to the Community, British and Danish ministers and parliamentarians tend to see disadvantage in major public debates about the nature of the Community. Especially in Denmark, but also to some extent in Britain, there is a lack of public discussion of the 'supra-national' aspects of Community life. Ministers declare flatly, and correctly, that there is no question of any early move towards federation. But they do not often explain why, in order to deal with common problems of the environment or to promote the competitiveness of European industry through the creation of a single great market, it is necessary each year to do things which involve sharing more sovereignty with our Community partners. Only rarely do they highlight the fact that, in order to make the Community work properly, it is sometimes necessary not to press some national interest in return for similar restraint by others. Though the British Government is in fact working at least as effectively as any other government for the unity of the internal market and the unity of the Community in the world, British ministers (except for Sir Geoffrey Howe and one or two others) have sometimes sounded grudging about the goal of 'European Union' to which their colleagues on the Continent attach great political importance. The anti-Marketeers make inaccurate remarks about the Community in Parliament and outside, and stand largely uncorrected.

From the point of view of getting our way even more often in the Council, it would be helpful if the British Government could achieve a gradual improvement in our European reputation. To this end they should perhaps explain to Parliament and people more often the need for joint action in the Community and why that does involve some sharing of sovereignty and proclaim their commitment to real progress towards the 'ever-closer union' of which the Treaty of Rome speaks, or even to the 'European Union' to which all successive British governments have committed themselves many times since 1972. That does not mean abolishing the monarchy, accepting the aim of creating a Federal Government or even agreeing that Community laws shall be passed without our consent. It means going on doing what we have been doing, but relating this to the goal of 'union'.

To get your way in the Council, you need a lot of skill, willpower and persistence. We have them, and others would say we do rather well. But the unique thing about the Community is that it is not just a permanent negotiation, not just another layer of government where national politics are ever-present, it is also a common enterprise in which hard-bitten ministers and officials from other countries *believe*. It is a matter of faith. And they mind if Britons suggest that their declarations of faith are empty rhetoric.

There may be no agreement among those around the European Council table about exactly where the Community is journeying to and at what speed. I suspect that many of them do not give this question serious thought, even once a year. But they know in their bones that we are all journeying together towards real European unity and it pains them if one of their number makes speeches suggesting that it will never happen and that they are not sincere.

Some British 'Europeans' believe that Britain has been a bad member. I do not accept that. If pressed, most of my opposite numbers in Brussels would almost certainly agree. To reassure myself before writing this paragraph, I asked one of them, an old Community hand from a very 'Communautaire' country, the straight question and he replied: 'Certainly not since 1979 – and we should have settled the budget question years before we did'. But even some of these same old hands, who have seen the British working con-structively in the Council, have an instinctive feeling that the British people are not really comfortable on the journey we are making together. It would do us a lot of good if this feeling came to be dispelled.

POLITICS

There has seldom been a moment since 1973 when there was not some Community issue at the centre of controversy in Britain and quite often the issue of Community membership itself has been revived. During the years of the present Conservative government, however, the controversy has settled to a more routine level. Even the new 'own resources' decision, putting the Fontainebleau agreement on the British budget problem and the increase in the VAT ceiling to 1.4% into Community legislation, only caused a relatively brief flurry of debate in the House of Commons.

Naturally both the Commons and the Lords take a close interest in an organisation which shares with them the right to make laws in the United Kingdom. The Lords has produced a long series of excellent reports on almost every aspect of Community life, copies of which I have often seen on the desks of Commissioners and officials in Brussels. By general consent, they are among the best analyses of Community policies available anywhere. The House of Commons has its Scrutiny Committee which goes carefully through all the draft legislation proposed by the Commission, with an explanatory memorandum from the British government department concerned, and recommends key issues for debate in the House itself. The government cooperates very fully with the Scrutiny Committee and does its best to ensure that even on urgent matters decisions are not taken in the Council while matters are still under scrutiny. The Permanent Representative is quite frequently instructed to put down a Parliamentary or Scrutiny Reserve on some item of business which has the effect of holding it up until the Scrutiny Committee has completed its work or, where they recommend this, a Parliamentary debate has taken place at home. Provided that delays do not have serious practical consequences and are not too long, the other members of the Community are understanding.

The other parliaments in the Community (apart from the Danish Folketing) do not seem to show a similar determination to keep tabs on their Executives. The Danes go much further still and their Parliamentary Committee meets every Friday to give a 'mandate' to the government for the Council meetings in the week ahead. This tends to make it very difficult for Denmark to negotiate in the Council, especially if new solutions are invented to problems during the debate itself, and has contributed to Denmark's isolation on many issues.

Fourteen years after Britain joined the Community, British Government and Parliamentary procedures seem therefore, at least for the time being, to have settled into a practical and sensible mould. There are still a few Conservative MPs who do not easily reconcile themselves to membership and perhaps more Labour MPs who see it as being incompatible with the policies they would like to pursue. But it seems reasonable to hope that Britain's membership will not be an issue which is raised directly in the next British general election.

There is a risk that it could become an issue again indirectly, because certain lines of economic policy would be incompatible with membership. As the history of steel, coal and shipbuilding in the 1980s shows, the Community does not interpret the rules on state aids inflexibly. Where there is a good case for temporary aids while restructuring takes place, the Commission will be helpful. But any policy based on massive state aids (which the Commission did not find to be compatible with the Treaty) or on reflation behind barriers to imports from the Community would almost certainly come to grief.

Unemployment is high throughout the Community, lower than in Britain in France and Germany, but higher than in Britain in, for example, the Netherlands and Spain. If a British Government were to impose controls on imports from other Community countries or to contravene the provisions of the Treaty on state aids, they would be seen by other member states not just as 'non-communautaire' – acting in breach of the letter and spirit of their Treaty obligations and of the principles of the Community – but as attempting to export British unemployment to their partners who already have quite enough of it. Before taking such action, the Government would have to think through its political and economic implications.

If the British Government were in the Commission's view in breach of the Treaty, they would, with the support of other member states, be bound to proceed against them in the European Court of Justice. If the Court found against the British Government, the Government's measures would be in breach of the European Communities Act 1972, and liable to challenge in the British courts by any company or individual whose interests were being damaged by them. British courts under that Act would be oliged to find in accordance with the judgments of the European Court. Defiance of the European Court's ruling would thus require difficult and controversial legislation in Parliament to set aside the European Communities Act. It would also provoke retaliation by other member countries. British membership of the Community would almost inevitably begin to unravel, whether or not that was a consequence intended or foreseen by the British Government. The United Kingdom's trading and economic activity and the legislative framework within which it is conducted have become so interwoven with those of its partners in the Community that the implications for the British economy, as well as for the demands on Parliament to pass legislation, would be literally incalculable.

The conclusion I draw is that it is not just a stated intention to leave the Community which would prove dangerous for the country. Any commitment to take action contrary to the Treaty would be liable to lead to the same difficulties before very long.

It would be a grave setback for Britain in the Community to have such a crisis, even if in the end it resulted in a British U-turn and a gradual resumption of relatively constructive membership. What Britain needs in order to ensure that its interests are best protected and promoted in the Council is steady normal Community behaviour for a decade. Since Fontainebleau we have been able to work constructively with most other member states on different issues.'

Even with our ancient rivals, the French, there are now more issues on which we see eye to eye than on which we differ. We could, with luck, soon transcend our past reputation of being a difficult member.

Unfortunately, it is only too probable that 'life itself' (as the Russians say when they mean something outside their own control) will make this ideal state of affairs hard to achieve, possibly even before the next British elections. Britain may well shortly find itself battling alone in another good cause and making itself still more unloved in the process. It is now only too likely, because the cost of the CAP continues to run out of control, that Britain will soon be asked to agree to additional funds for the Community budget. Whenever this happens the British Government of the day seems bound to raise serious objections, even if the other governments are ready to confirm, or even improve on the Fontainebleau agreement, and thus to keep the British VAT share well below that of other member governments. In my own view, the only option that makes sense, in the Community's own interest as well as our own, will be to insist that the CAP is put on a basis which is viable in the long term before increasing the money available to the Community again. To allow the Community budget more money while leaving the CAP as it is would only be to postpone the crisis for a year or two and to ensure that it was still more difficult to deal with then.

General de Gaulle's Foreign Minister, M. Couve de Murville, was once quoted as saying (during a period of intense French isolation) 'Je ne suis jamais seul, lorsque j'ai raison' (I'm never alone when I'm right). I would not want to encourage any British minister to take a leaf out of his book by glorifying isolation and it certainly would not be Sir Geoffrey Howe's style to do so. But I do believe that it may be necessary to endure a further period of isolation and criticism in order finally to get the CAP put on a sensible basis. No one else, alas, is likely to do it for us.

9

The Media

THE MEDIA ARE an integral part of the Community process. There is a large and professional press corps resident in Brussels. Whenever some event attracts public attention, the television teams descend *en masse* from all over the world. Several times during my years in Brussels, the Foreign Secretary and his advisers have almost had to fight their way through the television cameras to get to the meeting-rooms. Something like one thousand journalists come to each meeting of the European Council.

Delegations constantly brief the press on and off the record. They pay special attention to their own national media because ministers are of course greatly interested in the way in which their actions in Brussels are reported at home. This can have significant internal political consequences for good or evil. But they also brief the press from other countries before important meetings and on-the-record press conferences are naturally open to all. Quite a lot of the time of a Permanent Representative is devoted to the media, briefing off-the-record before Council meetings, giving off-the-record interviews to visiting journalists, including prominent Americans, giving occasional on-the-record interviews to foreign newspapers and appearing from time to time on Belgian or even French Television or radio. But it is of course primarily ministers on whom the burden of informing the media falls and they spend a lot of time on this during their visits to Brussels, apart from the on-the-record press conferences that they normally give towards the end of each Council.

The primary emphasis in all this activity is on providing the press with a clear picture of what is actually going on. They have many sources, not all of whom tell exactly the same story all the time. In my view there is a premium on giving the press accurate and objective information. No one can get away for long with misleading them. But naturally ministers from all countries wish to present their own policies in the best possible light and so, when there is an unresolved argument in the Council, different ministers put across conflicting views and even when there is agreement it is not unknown for more than one of them to cry Victory for themselves rather than to say that all have gained from the compromise reached. Finally, from time to time, one or other delegation may use the press as part of a negotiating ploy, to worry their negotiating adversary by running a new proposal as a diversion or to stress some relatively unimportant point in order to cover a move on what really matters. Most of what happens in the Commission and the Council becomes known. The journalists work on the ground floor of the Council building and have many friends among the delegations. *Agence-Europe*, a daily information sheet, has such good sources that it is able to publish the contents of closed-door debates in Commission, Council and even COREPER. The Community believes in open government and everyone acts on the assumption that their position in negotiation will become known to the media. Only when the Permanent Representatives meet alone without advisers or interpreters, in order to discuss something in confidence, is there any chance that a delicate question, such as an appointment to a Community post, can be settled in private.

There is therefore masses of material for the press to work on. The trouble is that very little of it is the stuff of which an article in the popular press can be made. So the popular press purveys a distorted and peculiar picture of the Community. Though the distortions are different in each country, the general level of misinformation is about the same. How could it be otherwise? If the Heads of Governments meet or the Finance Ministers have a well-publicised verbal clash, the popular press naturally feels the need to include something – but that something is usually so over simplified as to be barely recognisable and often conveyed in national championship terms. 'Maggie battles!' Even the correspondents of the serious newspapers often have trouble getting their papers to print the whole of an adequate explanation of a complicated Council decision. Those from the popular press know they would have no chance.

Sub-editors are another major hazard. Let us take the example of the Commission proposal to permit British and Danish chocolate, which has always been allowed to contain a percentage of non-cocoa vegetable fats when sold at home, now to be sold in other countries which have hitherto insisted on 100% cocoa. When the proposal was discussed in the European Parliament, some Belgian, German and French MEPs objected, perhaps because there were vested interests involved, and suggested that if British chocolate were to be sold in the Continent, it should be called Vegolate. By the time the story got into the popular press, even if the body of the article was not actually misleading, the headlines read something like: 'EEC. British chocs to be Vegolate.'

To take another example, MEPs discussed the teaching of history in different countries. There is a real problem. It is hard sometimes even to detect that British and French history books are recounting the same wars, so much do they both concentrate on the battles they won and not those they lost. A French MEP pointed out the difficulties of trying to avoid nationalist manifestations about the past and in the course of his argument said that, if this were to be carried to its logical conclusion, the British would have to rename Trafalgar Square and Waterloo Station and the French the Gare d'Austerlitz. The popular press expressed outrage at a 'French proposal' that these famous British places be renamed because of the Community! Those who want to present the Community in a bad light naturally take advantage of these possibilities.

Even where distortion on this scale is not involved, sub-editors can produce headlines which mislead. Commission proposals for legislation have of course to be examined by the European Parliament (which has to give an opinion) and by Working Groups of representatives of member governments, by COREPER, and Council before they can be adopted. But they are often headlined as though all these processes had been completed and the proposal adopted as soon as the Commission send it forward. In the real world, if the proposal is not a good one, it will never pass.

The serious newspapers (of which the *Financial Times* is perhaps the most read of all in the Community institutions, with *Le Monde* close behind it) give wide coverage to the important discussions. But the role even of the serious newspapers is not in practice always helpful to presenting the Community in an objective and constructive light.

Newspapers like a good row, a battle between clashing ministers. It is in fact very rare indeed for voices to be raised or tempers lost in the Council. But the popular press regularly proclaims, for example, that 'Maggie is furious' and even the serious press often reports major clashes on its front pages when all that has happened is a reasoned argument about means, not ends.

On such matters, the ordinary newspaper reader gains his impression from the headlines in his own newspaper. He does not know that in many cases clashes reported on its front page provide a highly-coloured account of one Council meeting, one brief discussion in a long process of reaching agreement. If the argument in question is subsequently resolved and agreement reached at the Council the following month, and unless the subject has real political sex appeal, the agreement will be reported, if at all, in a few lines on an inside page, perhaps the business news. The ordinary reader may not even relate the one

127

event to the other. So his picture of constant bickering continues unclouded by the settlement.

In presenting Community debates to the media, ministers have a serious problem of different audiences. For British and, still more, Danish ministers who have anti-Market forces at home to contend with, this is a particular difficulty. But it applies in other member states as well. At home they wish to be reported as having been tough and having fought vigorously and successfully for national interests. In the Community they need to be seen to have worked for compromise, paid attention to the interests of other member states and put the need for agreement first. They have probably done both these things, but it is not easy to put them both across at the same time in a press conference. This, and the need to defend negotiating positions to the hilt in public until those parts of them which are known to be going to have to be discarded have actually been discarded, makes the process of negotiating almost in public, as ministers do in the Community, very difficult to present to the media.

From time to time, the Presidency of the day or some other Minister points out to his colleagues that the Community has been getting an undeservedly poor press recently. Or an ambassador complains discreetly at a COREPER lunch about the way a minister from another country has misrepresented his own government's position. A good resolution is then taken to avoid Euro-pessimism, to draw the attention of the press to A-points containing significant agreements, to take care in referring to the position of other Delegations – and so on. But the results are short-lived. Ministers and officials are too busy solving their problems to remember to take trouble with the presentation of debates and decisions to the media, except of course to make sure that their own national press understands how well their own delegation has done in pursuit of the national interest!

Whatever happens, there will always be controversy about the Community in the media. It is inevitable and healthy that there should be. It is not a sign of disunity that ministers argue in the Council, even though the media may exaggerate the ferocity of the arguments. It is not a sign that the Community is not working if agreement on a complex issue is reached at the second, third or fourth Council meeting and that meanwhile fierce arguments are reported. It does not mean that the Community is in disarray if five or even ten major arguments on different subjects are reported from the different Councils each month. What all these things mean is that the Community is intensely alive and dealing with a very large number of complicated issues which are important from both a political and economic point of view.

128

There is no less controversy in Washington, a federal capital, than there is in Brussels. American ministers argue with each other, even in public; the President and the Congress can be at loggerheads; even the Supreme Court gets drawn into controversy. It would be absurd to expect that the business of the European Community could always get done in perfect harmony. Paradoxically the more the effort put into the unity of the internal market or the unity of the Community in the world, the more the controversy. This is a point which needs constantly to be made to all those whose gut reaction is that life in the Council is more like the survival of the fittest in the prehistoric jungle than the uniting of a civilized continent in a twentieth-century world. Politics, whether at local, national or Community level, is hardly ever pure sweetness and light.

10

National Characteristics and Interests. Enlargement

SEVERAL RECENT CHAPTERS have been Anglocentric. It is time to take a look at the other members, their special concerns, and their national charateristics as they manifest themselves in the Community. Of course, the angle of vision is still British. It is hard for it to be otherwise in an ex-Permanent Representative. But I shall try to paint a picture in which the others would recognise themselves without caricature.

Of course, we must not exaggerate the differences in behaviour of the different nationalities. There are Germans who have characteristics often thought of as Italian, and Englishmen with characteristics thought to be French. But most old Community hands would agree that each nationality produces patterns of behaviour which repeat themselves. Member countries' interests within the Community are rather more divergent than their behaviour. But even here it is important not to exaggerate. The differences on internal Community questions are not of so serious a kind as to be irreconcilable through the usual Community processes and the differences in their interests in the outside world are relatively minor. It is definitely not true that differences in national characters and interests are so acute as to make the Community unworkable.

France

Founder-members, very difficult in the Community during the Gaullist period, tenacious, and usually at the centre of most Community negotiations, arch-negotiators, the French get their way even more often than their economic and political weight would justify. As seen from the outside, they have not since 1981 been as well co-ordinated as they were in the 1970s, mainly because their co-ordinating body, the SGCI, has not of late been so much at the centre of things as it was, for example, under President Pompidou. But it may also be because each minister and his 'cabinet' have been rather more prone to ploughing their own furrow. The French are only occasionally ready to negotiate below the level of the Council. Nevertheless on any given subject it is usually possible to find a French official or minister with whom business can be done, except just before a European Council, when no one wishes to commit the President to any particular line of action.

France has so many interests that it is hard to single any out for special mention. Drawing a bow at a venture, some of their key concerns seem to be the interests of small farmers in the South and West, protecting the CAP against American offensives, relations with the Mediterranean and French African countries and containing the growth of the French net contribution to the budget. They like to be seen to be working with the Germans to keep the Community show on the road. They are at the non-Federalist end of the spectrum, quite close to the British, with the Danes in the extreme position.

It is rare to find a French official who is not at the top end of scale as far as intelligence and Community skills are concerned. If they have a fault, and not all of them have, it is that they subscribe too often to the conspiracy theory of history and of Community negotiation. Perhaps this is because they themselves believe on occasion in confusing the negotiating parties about their real aims.

Germany

Founder-members, now more prone to punch their full weight, but still seldom as assertive as the French, the Germans have from time to time made themselves quite unpopular, usually by being difficult about authorizing Community expenditure. Considering that their net contribution to the budget is two to three times that of Britain, this is not surprising. But they are not always helpful and persuasive about it.

The Germans would agree that they are not as well co-ordinated as the French or British, have difficulty in getting agreement in Bonn to a negotiating position and even more difficulty thereafter in changing it. This is partly a function of having a coalition government, partly due to the Federal character of the German system and to the division of responsibility (as a result of a deal done by Adenauer with Erhardt in the early days) between the Economic Ministry (nominally in charge of co-ordination) and the others, particularly the Finance Ministry. This makes it harder than with most other governments to predict where the German position will finally settle or to negotiate points with them well in advance.

131

They too have a very wide range of interests. Among the most salient seem to be preventing wasteful expenditure, *but* without damage to small Bavarian farmers; fighting protectionism in the Community and the world but without offending France; proper management of European/American relations; avoiding erosion of their special trade arrangements with East Germany; action to protect their forests; and pushing the Community forward, if possible with France. They are in principle more Federation-minded than the French, but may have now joined the Luxembourg Compromise camp (France, the UK, Denmark, Greece, Ireland, and perhaps Spain and Portugal) by vetoing any decline in cereal prices in Germany in the 1985 price-fixing.

German influence in the Community is second only to that of French, which is not surprising in view of the size and strength of their economy and the fact that they are its main paymaster. If they have a fault – and many of them do not – it is that they erect the free market into a question of ideology and forget that all free markets have to operate in a known and accepted framework. As Lord Lever, no mean expert on markets, once said to me: 'It is a well-known fact that the market in uncatalogued Rembrandts at auctions on Long Island on a wet Saturday night is far from perfect.' In theory, at least, some Germans want to behave as if all markets were not only free but perfect all the time.

The Franco-German Motor

Both countries attach great importance to being seen to be working together on the Community and, from time to time, take joint initiatives. But, despite a great deal of bilateral consultation at every level, it seems rather rare for the French and Germans to be working closely together in the Council on particular subjects. That is not to say that the Franco-German relationship is a fake. After all even in the best marriages there are irritations and clashes of interest as well as differences of opinion. Even where they have the most serious differences, which is quite often, they make an effort not to give too much of an impression of being at loggerheads. Common Franco-German pressure to achieve a specific result is not unknown and, when it happens, usually successful (the most significant example was the setting-up of the EMS in 1978). But it is much rarer than the ordinary newspaper reader would infer from the impression given each time French and German leaders meet for France and Germany to work actively together to promote a common line in the Council. This is just as well, because a Franco-German axis would be resented by the others.

Italy

Founder-members, usually able and successful negotiators on subjects dear to them, the Italians are among the most fulsome in their rhetorical support for 'European Union'. At the same time, they keep at least as sharp an eye to the main chance as anyone else. With less formal and visible co-ordinating machinery than the French, Germans or British, they nevertheless usually speak with one voice. Almost always full of charm, always on the look-out for a 'combinazione' which does Italy a bit of good as well as solves a problem, they have some very able officials as well as ministers.

Their main interests are promoting Community action on technology and research (the joint Research Centre is in Italy), seeing that the treatment of Mediterranean agriculture is no less favourable than that of Northern agriculture and protecting it from concessions to other countries. They succeeded in turning a net contribution to the budget in 1978 into a gain of around 1,500 million ECUs by 1984, partly through a skilful campaign on behalf of Mediterranean agriculture.

They are strong defenders and supporters of the European Parliament and at the Federalist end of the spectrum. Like the Benelux countries, Italy strongly dislikes any appearance of a Franco-German axis seeking to impose decisions on the Community and would be still more hostile towards any Franco-German-British triangle trying to do so.

Netherlands

Founder-members with well-balanced views, determined, usually playing a constructive role, they do not however forget to promote Dutch interests. Normally very well co-ordinated, despite the independent role of their Foreign Minister under their Constitution, they usually try to push decisions forward and are ready to negotiate below ministerial level. Across the board, the best linguists in the Community; almost all Dutch Ministers and officials seem to be able to operate effectively in English, French and German – which is no mean feat.

Though one of the two or three countries which benefit most per head from the CAP, their self-interest is sufficiently enlightened for them normally to be at the reforming end of the spectrum. Their other main interests seem to be keeping protectionism at bay, inside and outside the Community; completing the internal market, including liberalizing land and air transport; proper management of the Community's foreign relations, including those with the United States; keeping up the momentum of progress in the Community.

Their positions seem nearer to those of the United Kingdom than are those of most other member states and they were the strongest supporters of British entry in the 1960s and eary 1970s. But they profess themselves disappointed by Britain's performance since 1973. They work closely with Belgium and Luxembourg, though seldom to the point of having common negotiating positions, and for example hold a Benelux Heads of Government meeting before the European Council.

With Belgium they are towards the Federalist end of the spectrum but perhaps rather more pragmatic. They both object strongly to inner groupings of the bigger countries and for that reason are suspicious of decisions being taken at the annual summits of the seven largest industrialized countries (which include France, Germany, Italy and Britain), even though the President of the Commission is always there to represent the interests of the Community and its non-participant members. If the Dutch have a fault, it is that they are so determined, in thought and action, that just occasionally some of them verge towards obstinacy.

Belgium

Founder-members, as devoted to finding compromises in the Council as they are in their own difficult governmental decisions, always in the van when there is discussion about the Community progressing, they nevertheless manage to fight hard when Belgian interests are at stake. As the Council lives in their capital, their Permanent Representative carries a heavy burden in their internal co-ordination. They are strongly attached to making Brussels the capital of Community one day, but see the need to pursue the objective discreetly. They are supporters of the CAP and their farm lobby is powerful, particularly the sugar beet lobby; not as enlightened as the Dutch as far as CAP reform is concerned. Otherwise their concerns seem mainly to be Community concerns – such as promoting Community research or achieving compromises in difficult situations whenever they may arise. They are not however at the free market end of the internal market discussion, and seem considerably more protectionist than the Dutch. Towards the Federalist end of the spectrum on issues like majority voting or the powers of the European Parliament, they do not nevertheless advocate immediate and radical constitutional change. If the Belgians have a fault, it is perhaps that they are so keen on compromise that they are sometimes ready to advocate bad solutions in order to achieve it.

Luxembourg

The smallest member state by far, population just over 100,000, but by virtue of being a founder-member and working hard in the Community interest, they have an influence disproportionate to their economic weight.

They have the Court, the EIB (European Investment Bank), the Parliament Secretariat and a part of the Commission in Luxembourg and are ready to fight like tigers to keep them. One quarter of Council meetings take place there. Steel, banking (incipient competition for Switzerland and almost greater secrecy), and the CAP are their main interests, apart from keeping the Community working properly, in which no member has a more direct interest. Sandwiched between France and Germany with no traditional window on a wider world, they follow one or the other or Benelux on most international issues. But, as if to prove the lack of relationship between size and competence, their 1985 Presidency was remarkably successful and they showed great skill and determination in bringing the negotiations on treaty changes to a conclusion.

Ireland

The new member who settled most easily into the Community, Ireland is a major beneficiary of the CAP and the Regional Fund, and gets over 5% of GNP from the Community budget. Until the advent of Greece, and now Spain and Portugal, by far the poorest member at almost 50% of average GNP-per-head, Ireland will probably have to work harder in future to maintain her benefits in competition with the newer members, particularly with Portugal which is almost half as poor again. Primarily interested in agriculture, above all in milk, Ireland is deeply concerned by the CAP's troubles, yet feels unable to support many of the measures of reform proposed. They have been quite successful in drawing in investment from outside the Community with liberal grants and the incentive of getting inside the Common Market.

Dr Fitzgerald is strongly in favour of rapid Community progress, though Ireland is usually at about the mid-point of the debate on constitutional issues and continues to support and use the Luxembourg Compromise, e.g. over milk quotas in 1984. The Irish neither align themselves consistently with (or against) any other member state nor seek to play a major role except on issues of direct concern to them.

Denmark

The Danish Government of the day sold the Community to the Danish people in 1972 as a purely economic organisation and successive Danish Ministers have been suffering the consequences of this false bill of sale ever since. Despite having consistently done extremely well out of the Community because of the efficiency and weight of Danish agriculture, Danish public opinion remains seriously split and active anti-Market forces are the strongest in any member. Many Danes feel more comfortable in a cosy Scandinavian setting than in the Community.

Their Parliament supervises every important Council negotiation through its Market Committee and the majority is consistently hostile in principle to the smallest move towards additional sharing of sovereignty. For all these reasons, Danish ministers, despite the present Government's relatively pro-European colour, find themselves in quite frequent difficulties in Brussels, where those who are isolated are expected to compromise. These difficulties came to a head over the Treaty amendment which other Heads of Government were ready to accept in Luxembourg in December, 1985; and it needed a referendum (won 56:44) for the Danes to remind themselves that the Community is good for them and that they have no choice but to play the Community game in a constructive way.

Agriculture and fisheries are the two subjects where Danish interests are most involved and on which they negotiate toughly and well. They also are strong defenders of free trade inside and outside the Community and continue to work hard for closer EEC/EFTA relations. On many subjects they feel closer to Britain than to most other members, though paradoxically they were one of our most ferocious opponents on the British budget problem. This was no doubt a function of their hostility to the very idea of computing net contributions and benefits, being both one of the biggest net beneficiaries in ECUs per head as well as having the highest GNP per head, the two statistics not sitting particularly well together under the public gaze.

Greece

Before Spain and Portugal, the last to enter, on 1st January, 1981, Greece has still not fully adapted to Community membership. Indeed, Mr Papandreou having come to power shortly after Greek entry with an equivocal policy towards membership, it has only recently become certain that Greece is in for good. The Greek economy is still adapting to membership (and recovering from poor economic policies), many Community laws are not yet respected and the implications of membership as far as common action in the world is concerned seem not to have been taken on board. Greece has had a consistently poor record in political co-operation.

Despite all this, the Greeks are sharp and successful negotiators and have secured for themselves a major Community loan (1.75 billion ECUs) to help with their balance of payments problems, yet another year's delay in introducing VAT, permission temporarily to have an import deposit scheme, as well as about 1,000 million ECUs a year in overall net benefits from the Community budget. Their Community policy seems to be very directly under Mr Papandreou's control and there is plenty of evidence that he is now, not surprisingly, reconciled to Community membership, even if it may take a little longer before Greece's position becomes less idiosyncratic.

RECONCILING NATIONAL INTERESTS

The extraordinary, and encouraging, thing about the Community is that, despite these differences of national characteristics and interests, ministers and officials not only manage to get problems solved but usually do so in an amicable way. Members of COREPER defend their national position, but take pride in contributing to agreement. Ministers seldom quarrel in private as the headlines would have us believe. The people who work in the Community have mostly lived there for so long that they have absorbed a Community culture which coexists with their national characteristics and makes it easier for them to edge forward to agreement together.

Both British and French friends of mine have from time to time asked me whether it is really possible for the two nations to overcome the antagonisms of the past and the differences in their interests and national characteristics enough to be able to work together in a united Europe. My answer has always been an unqualified yes; and I am happy to say that, since Fontainebleau, I have seen the French and the British working together as closely as any other two countries in the Community. This did not surprise me, though some of our colleagues seemed to find it odd and amusing when my old friend and adversary from the great budget battles of the early 1980s, Ambassador Luc de Nanteuil, returned to COREPER after a three year absence in January 1985, and kept agreeing with me – and I with him. France and Britain were doing business together normally and the others soon came to recognise that. If Community 'warfare' breaks out again over the cost of the CAP, our successors will no doubt have again to do battle for a time. But the truth is that, across the whole spread of Community work, Britain and France have now a great deal in common, including our similar net contributions to the budget.

Allowances have to be made for national characteristics in conducting Community negotiations. The very stuff of those negotiations is the reconciliation of conflicting interests in such a way that there is a collective gain, and no serious losses. Agreement is not easy. But let no one tell you that it is impossible. It almost always comes in the end.

SPAIN AND PORTUGAL. THE LAST TO ENTER

The diversity of the interests and characteristics of the Ten showed up very clearly in the complex and difficult negotiations for Spanish and Portuguese entry into the Community. For example, France was determined to protect producers of wine and vegetables in South-West France from Spanish competition for as long as possible. The Netherlands (among others) was keen to open up the Spanish market for Northern agricultural products as quickly as possible. Italy strongly resisted moves to impose action to deal with the olive oil surplus in the enlarged Community as part of the entry negotiations. Britain wanted to get the very high Spanish tariff on cars down quickly to produce fairer competition with the Spanish cars now being exported to Britain in large quantities. The main fishing countries (UK, Denmark, France, Ireland, and Germany) were determined to protect their interests under the Common Fisheries Policy, while Italy was, understandably, ready to be more relaxed.

I only give a few examples. Literally hundreds of detailed questions had to be dealt with in the Accession Treaties, which were far more complicated than those of the first enlargement (Britain, Ireland, Denmark) simply because there is now so much more Community law to accept and adapt to.

The negotiations took too long and there were times when some people speculated that the will to complete them simply was not there. It is true that in several countries some quite powerful voices were raised against Spanish and Portuguese entry. There were those who feared Spanish agricultural competition, even in a few cases industrial competition. There were those who did not wish to add two more relatively poor countries and were worried about the cost of helping Spain and, especially, Portugal. There were those who foresaw increased difficulties in making decisions and the risk of the Community turning into another OECD.

There were, however, those who reckoned they stood to gain from opening up the Iberian markets. Under the EEC/Spain agreement of 1970, which was not supposed to last all this time, Spanish tariffs remained relatively high, seven or eight times the Community tariff for cars, for example. The advantages for many industries in the Community of Ten of cutting Spanish tariffs will be considerable. They will be halved in three years and eliminated in seven. But it was for broad political reasons that majority opinion in all the governments held steadily to the view that Spanish and Portuguese entry was necessary and that the attendant costs and risks must be accepted. Article 237 of the Treaty says that 'any European state' may apply to join. During the 1970s it came to be accepted that this meant any *democratic* European state. Spain and Portugal became democratic and applied to join. The Ten agreed in 1977/78 to open entry negotiations and remained united in wanting the negotiations to succeed.

And so, after a painful last heave and much lost sleep in the spring of 1985, the entry negotiations were completed, despite all the complications, just in time to allow all concerned to ratify the Accession Treaties before 1st January 1986, thus enlarging the Community for the third time on that day.

That must have been the right outcome. No doubt Spanish and Portuguese membership will create some difficulties in the next few years. Interpretation with nine languages, i.e. nine by nine, will be more troublesome and expensive. The entry terms were fairly tough and there will be pressure from some groups, such as Spanish fishermen and farmers, to renegotiate them. The Community's internal decisions will be a little more difficult to take and its unity in the world temporarily less well focussed. There will be a risk of a North/South, rich/poor division and therefore some added controversy in the Council.

But how could a Community which claims to be becoming 'European Union' and to speak for Europe in the world turn away two old European States, now young democracies, who applied to join in the proper way and were ready to assume the obligations of membership? To have rejected them would have been to divide Western Europe and her adversaries would have exploited her division. Morever, in a broad sense, Spain and Portugal help to complete Europe. For Latin America in particular this will be important.

It is fashionable among anti-marketeers to say that the third enlargement is to be welcomed because, together with the second (Greece), it will put paid to the hopes of those who want Europe to go on uniting. To think this is to misunderstand the processes of the Community. Perhaps one small reason why English-speaking people, even more than others, find those processes difficult to grasp is that we have no single word for *engrenage* – literally the process of cogs meshing together, but used to convey the idea that once something or someone has been drawn into the machine, the cogs will continue to turn and

139

draw them in further still. Spain, and Portugal, and even Greece, will become part of the *engrenage*. Perhaps the machine will work less fast and less smoothly for a while. But I do not believe for a moment that it will grind to a halt.

This may be the place to treat, in passing, the idea of a 'two-speed' Europe or 'differentiation'. Of course, not all twelve countries can or should do everything together. Luxembourg will not have a fishing fleet. Greece, and to a lesser extent Italy and France, may benefit from special Integrated Mediterranean programmes. This or that country should for a time be allowed, if the circumstances demand it, a special derogation from a Community law. Britain and Greece may stay outside the exchange rate mechanism of the EMS for a while longer. Outside the Community, firms from four or five countries may make a civilian or military aircraft. In brief, flexibility is required.

But even with Twelve, the normal rule must surely be that Community law applies to all and that exceptions are temporary; that the Community budget is financed by all out of 'own resources', even if special spending programmes are devised for certain countries; and that the Community acts internationally as one, even if just occasionally some country is permitted a special position. To go beyond this in the direction of 'differentiation' would be to risk turning it into fragmentation.

The title of this section, 'The last to enter', is deliberately ambiguous. Have the last two new members completed the Community family? Probably not in the long run. But one thing is certain; it will be best if there are no more enlargements for quite a long time to allow Greece, still half out, and Spain and Portugal, to become thoroughly run in.

There seems a good chance that there will be a long pause. Among the remaining democratic European countries, Norway may join one day, but will hardly apply in the next decade. Sweden, Austria and Switzerland will continue, perhaps for longer still or always, to feel inhibited by their neutrality. Only Turkey and just conceivably Cyprus or Malta, seem at all likely to put themselves forward.

Turkey is an important country and has a key position in the NATO Alliance. Though only a small fraction of their country is in continental Europe, the Turks would be much offended if anyone were to suggest that they be told they were not European. The Turkish Government has made serious progress on the human rights front and it would be a mistake to say, as a majority of the European Parliament might, that they are not quite democratic. The Greeks should restrain themselves from saying that they would veto their old enemy. But in my opinion the Turkish economy will need many more years of good management before they could sensibly think of assuming the obligations of membership. Portugal, a poor country with few industries and a backward agriculture, may well suffer rather a lot from adapting to membership. Still poorer Turkey, a vast country which could not possibly hope to receive similar help in terms of resource transfers per head, would find the process unacceptably painful. So it would be best for all concerned to wait a while before considering full membership for Turkey.

Meanwhile the Twelve, besides being an auspicious number, can be said to include all the traditional Western European cultures and to represent the vast majority of Western European people. It was perhaps presumptuous of the Six, or even the Nine, to speak of the Community as though it was Europe. Anti-marketeers, purists and friends of Eastern Europe may continue to complain about the Twelve calling themselves Europe. But when we talk of Europe's importance in the history of our millennium, especially the cultural history, it is primarily about developments in the Twelve that we are thinking. The Twelve are not far from representing the Continent of Europe as we normally conceive of it.

11

Europe and the Rest of the World

A GREAT DEAL of good but often unrecognised work is done on the Community's external policy and on taking common positions in foreign policy outside the Community domain through political co-operation. As a result, Europe is perceived in many parts of the world to be more united than it feels itself to be. I found this particularly noticeable, before I went to Brussels as Permanent Representative, when I had to travel widely as Deputy Under-Secretary in charge of economic affairs. Those I met in Washington, Delhi, Tokyo or Peking did not ask me about the British position on world economic issues but about that of the Community. What the Community might do in international economic negotiations could well determine the outcome, but not what Britain or France or Germany might do, unless part of a common Community position.

But the full potential of European unity is still not being exploited. Some European politicians act from time to time (but still more speak) as though they could influence world events on their own. Too often, as on President Reagan's Strategic Defence Initiative (SDI) European governments go different ways without first consulting and giving careful thought to the pros and cons of taking a common position. It is not good politics in France or Britain to react to the world's events by saying that the influence even of the larger European countries on their own is limited, and that a European position must be worked out before anything else is done. But the truth is that foreign policy initiatives by individual European countries are often based on an illusion – or home politics – and cannot be expected to influence events to the same extent as a Community initiative.

Of course, some member states have special links with, and influence in, different parts of the world, for example, France with Francophone Africa or Belgium with Zaire, Britain with some but far from all its ex-colonies round the world, Germany with Turkey, Greece with Cyprus, Italy with Malta – to quote only a few. The foreign policy of the Community should aim to enhance these relationships and draw advantage from them, and certainly avoid undermining them. But no member state has a sufficient network of special links for it to be able to base an independent foreign policy on them.

As the world gets smaller and television brings the dramas on the other side of the world into European living-rooms and home politics, ministers find that they have to take positions – in Parliament, on television and in the UN and elsewhere. They are strongly tempted to say what will go down well at home, whether or not it will influence events. This will not change, but if Europe is to increase its influence its members will need to speak still more often and more nearly with one voice.

We are halfway to a common policy already. In political cooperation the Foreign Ministries of the Twelve are in constant touch, in person, by telephone and by telex. Those responsible for each region and especially for areas of tension meet regularly, compare notes on what is going on and try to thrash out a common attitude. Compared with fifteen years ago, when political cooperation began, a lot of progress has been made towards a common data base and a common analysis of the facts. The importance of this factor should not be underestimated. When some dramatic event takes place and the ministers in each country have to make statements, the advice they get from their officials about its significance will now generally be quite similar.

It is true that the Twelve collectively, in political cooperation, are not immune from the disease from which they suffer nationally of making statements for statements' sake and without real attention to the question of what effect, if any, they will have on the situation and the countries directly involved. Press, Parliament and public opinion expect the Foreign Ministers and Heads of Government when they meet to react to events in Afghanistan, South Africa, Poland, Central America, or the Middle East. And so draft statements are prepared, approved and issued. Some of these statements, such as the Venice Declaration on the Middle East made by the Heads of Government in June 1980, have had a significant, if still marginal, effect on events in the area. Many others have evaporated with the breath of the Presidency spokesman who uttered them to the press. It is hard for it to be otherwise. Even the United States, much more directly involved and with real leverage on Israel, has made many statements these last five years which have changed nothing. But the right rule must surely be, as Mrs Thatcher stressed at each European Council, only to issue statements when there is something new to say and when there is some chance of them having a useful effect.

Ministers, meeting in political cooperation, quite often engage in more practical and traditional diplomacy. For example, they depute the Foreign

Minister of the Presidency or a Troika (past, present and future Presidencies) to represent the Community in discussion with a group of countries (e.g. the Contadora Group in its search for peace in Central America) or to visit a country and report back, e.g., South Africa in August 1985. In addition, the Prime Ministers and Foreign Ministers of the Presidency often speak in the name of the Community as well as their own when, for example, visiting the United States during their tour of office, as British Ministers will no doubt do in the second half of 1986. All these activities, as well as putting the Community as such on the diplomatic map and making other countries aware of Europe's gradual move towards a common foreign policy, have some influence on the way other countries think about and deal with the international problems they face. Also in political co-operation, the Twelve take common positions in international organisations on subjects outside the strict scope of the Treaty of Rome. Under the new Political Co-operation Treaty, approved at the Luxembourg European Council in December 1985, their obligations to consult with each other and to do their best to take common positions will be made formal, and a small secretariat established to provide continuity and to help the Presidency with running the political co-operation machinery.

Let us hope that this formal commitment will reduce the number of occasions when this or that member government – and almost all are guilty in varying degrees – shoots from the hip as soon as some target of opportunity appears in its field of vision, without considering whether what it does or says is likely to cause problems for its European partners or will influence events in the broad direction which would suit European interests. The more genuine consultation there is and, in consequence, the more the Twelve take a common position, the better the chance that European interests will be protected and promoted and the European contribution to peace-making effective.

On matters covered by the Treaty the unity of the Community has always been a legal requirement. Under Article 113, the Commission negotiates with other countries on all matters covered by the common commercial policy – in accordance with directives laid down by the Council and with the assistance of a committee of member governments (the 113 Committee).

This procedure, when it is working well, provides a powerful negotiating team. Since the Council has to agree on the Commission's mandate and since there are usually enough member states insisting on a tough opening line to get it accepted, the Commission's negotiating partners from other countries face a hard task. The Commission can only move towards them with the consent of a qualified majority in the 113 Committee and exploits this fact in negotiation.

When it thinks the time has come to make a move or to settle, it can usually get a majority of member states to back it as long as they think it has negotiated skilfully. Some of the world's best negotiators are to be found among the small number of senior officials in DG I, the Directorate-General in charge of external affairs (except for the Lomé Convention, food aid, and development policy, which have their own Directorate-General in DG VIII).

Even where the common commercial policy is not involved, member states seek to take common positions in international economic discussions under Article 116. On occasion, as for example in the so-called 'North/South dialogue' in Paris in 1976/77, the Community fields a single team even on matters outside direct Community competence and is then represented by the Presidency. In the final stages, the UK was in the Chair. Though the Community had first to meet to establish its own position and then join in coordinating a position of the industrialised countries with the US, Japan, Canada, Australia and others before negotiating with the developing countries, it was able to adopt at least as constructive a position as the US or Japan and came to occupy a pivotal position at the Conference. My own previous experience of North/South negotiations had been in UNCTAD before we joined the Community and it was very striking how many times more influence we had, with the US and with developing countries alike, as the representatives of the Community rather than of the UK.

On occasion, the instruments of the common commercial policy have been used for political purposes. For example, when the Polish authorities imposed martial law and cracked down on Solidarity, the Community took economic measures of a modest kind against the Soviet Union and Poland, as a sign of disapproval and a warning of the danger of a serious rupture in relations if repression became too severe and cruel. When the Argentines invaded the Falkland Islands in 1982, the Community imposed an immediate trade and arms embargo. On such an occasion, the ministers agree in political co-operation that measures need to be taken and in Council on the regulation to implement them, they themselves metaphorically wearing their political co-operation and their Council hats at different moments during the same meeting. All this causes Danish ministers, who have to continue to pretend that the Community is a purely economic organisation, a certain amount of embarrassment. They managed, for example, to persuade the Council to allow them to opt out of the application of the regulation adopted as a result of martial law in Poland on the understanding that they would apply equivalent measures under national legislation.

A great deal of work also goes into the Community's association arrange-

145

ments with ACP and Mediterranean Countries, group-to-group relations with, for example, ASEAN or Central America and bilateral agreements with many countries (briefly described in Chapter Two). Just as in private life you need to nourish and cultivate your friendships, even old ones, if they are not to fade and become insubstantial, so does a country or the Community itself need to work away at its international relationships. When things go well, as for example in the EEC/ASEAN example, there is little to write about in the newspapers. This does not mean the relationship is unimportant.

The interests of Community countries in the world are now extremely similar. France and Britain, for example, no longer fight each other for influence in the Levant as they were still doing, almost by reflex action, after the Second World War. Italy or Spain may want to pay more attention to Central America than Britain or Denmark, but our interests are the same – to contribute to a peaceful settlement of differences, to prevent the area from becoming a major scene of East/West conflict, and therefore to promote healthy economic development. With few exceptions the same is true wherever in the world you look.

The main exception is naturally commercial rivalry. National governments have become more, not less, involved in supporting the sales efforts of their 'national champion' companies. With France setting the pace, governments have increasingly (and in my view mistakenly) taken to competing with each other in 'mixed credit', i.e. bribing Third World countries to buy their products by reducing the price with an aid package. This rivalry will continue, except in so far as European companies come together in joint ventures or other forms of co-operation in order to meet the American and Japanese challenge. France, Britain and Germany have, for example, been known all to lobby foreign governments jointly or severally on behalf of the Airbus.

Secondary exceptions are issues on which only one member country has an interest which others do not share. The Danes, for example, have a strong interest in keeping the Greenlanders reasonably sweet despite Greenland opting out of the Community, while other member Governments, particularly the Germans, are more interested in getting favourable implementation of the Community's fishing agreement with Greenland. Another example is the issue of the Falklands in the UN. Other member governments think the UK would do well to talk to Argentina about all aspects of Anglo-Argentine relations, even if we have no intention of changing our line on the need to respect the will of the islanders to remain free of Argentina. They also wish to improve their own relations with Argentina. So they are unwilling to follow British wishes and vote against a mild Argentine resolution which does not prejudge the substance.

These exceptions do not contradict the main point which is that there is a broad consensus in the Community about the nature of Europe's relations with the rest of the world, with important reservations on the part of Greece. Of course, the broad consensus is not news and the exceptions are, but the consensus is much more important and extensive than the disagreements.

The Community are broadly agreed that transatlantic relations must be based on partnership (though the French have no word for it) and must therefore be handled in such a way that trade friction does not lead to a worsening confrontation which might affect the NATO alliance. Ireland, which is not a member of NATO and is jealous of her military neutrality, would agree with the whole of the last sentence except the last six words. Greece might hesitate to agree explicitly but does not contest common action on this basis.

It has not always been easy to maintain US/European relations on an even keel; and if protectionism continues to increase in Congress it will get distinctly difficult. There are grievances on both sides.

Europeans suspect the US Government of having hidden motives of commercial rivalry with Western Europe and Japan in the increasing rigour of American action to prevent the transfer of technology out of the US, in the name of denying it to the Soviet Union. They resent American efforts to enforce American law on the supposedly independent European subsidiaries of American companies, particularly since those same companies proclaim themselves to be European companies deserving to be treated just as favourably as any genuinely European company. The Community has made collective representations to the US Government on this sort of issue on several occasions.

Both the Community and the United States are committed to maintaining the GATT and the open trading system of the industrialized world. Both, incidentally, have a similar interest in reducing the huge Japanese trade surpluses by getting Japan to turn to a more normal ratio of imports of manufactures to GDP, though the US Administration has always been reluctant, for political and security reasons, to 'gang-up on Japan'. But protectionism is a disease which takes many insidious forms and supporters of the open trading system seem to find it much easier to recognize it in others than in themselves. Within the Community there is a spectrum of opinion on the subject, with France and Italy rather more protectionist than Germany, Holland or Denmark, with Britain nearly in the middle. But though these differences do give rise to some strong argument in the Council, they are usually resolved without too great difficulty or delay. The Germans are no more pure free traders than the French are out-and-out protectionists. Moreover when the Council meets to work out a common position vis-à-vis the US Government on some tricky trade issue, all the ministers know that they need to settle any remaining difficulties between their governments before they depart. Otherwise the Commission will be unable to act. For all of them it is better to have a common position which is not exactly what they wanted – but fairly near it – than none at all.

Europeans believe that the spirit of US trade legislation is contrary in some respects to the GATT. It allows, may even force, the President to ignore his GATT obligations. Some American measures, for example, compelling a reluctant European industry to make voluntary restraint arrangements (VRAs) to limit steel exports to America are felt to be high-handed and protectionist, even though the Community has been successfully twisting the arms of nearly twenty steel-supplying countries for five years to make them sign VRAs covering exports to the Community. Steel is a constant source of US/EC friction, but not the only one – wheat, milk products, citrus, pasta, wine, etc. also give trouble.

Americans dislike the Common Agricultural Policy as a whole with its Community preference, import levies, and guaranteed prices which limit US exports to the Community. But, above all, they resent the export subsidies which, they claim, are causing them to lose ground in their traditional markets for agricultural exports in Third World countries. In this, they are strongly supported by Australia and, less strongly, by New Zealand, whose favourable butter and lamb agreements with the Community are a restraint on their criticism of its policies. The Americans have been going over to the offensive with heavily subsidised sales of their own, for example to Egypt, which has caused the Community to respond by increasing their export restitutions to match the American subsidies. The Europeans argue that the Americans too give vast subsidies to their agriculture, even if they do it by rather different means; and, very aptly, that people in glass houses should not throw stones.

The rights and wrongs of these skirmishes in agricultural trade are neither absolute nor easily adjudicated. They arouse considerable passion when the skirmishes begin to look as though they may escalate into battles, still worse war. So far they have always been kept under control, but the risks are now greater as the surpluses and the stocks grow on both sides of the Atlantic and the farmers are less prosperous, particularly in the United States.

It is naturally those who deal with agriculture and trade who are in the front line in European-American discussions of these difficult issues, but the essential politico-strategic partnership is the backcloth against which they go on. There are hawks and doves on both sides and the doves have to help each other.

It is hard for the European dove to know where to draw the line. From the European point of view there can be no question of simply going quietly, however badly the Americans may behave. To do so would not only directly damage European interests, it would also remove a powerful argument from those in the United States who are working for a reasonable balance in the transatlantic relationship and who are pointing out that both sides would lose if trade war breaks out. The Commission and the member governments of the Community have therefore to play a careful game, firm but not totally inflexible. The Commission, especially the Belgian and Dutch Commissioners responsible for trade and agriculture, Declerq and Andriessen, carry a heavy load. An agricultural trade war between Europe and the United States would damage both sides with especially serious consequences for the Community budget.

A huge effort has been made by both sides in recent years to keep communications open and where differences are too difficult to settle to find mechanisms for handling them. Panels in the GATT to study particular problems have proved useful. Commission and US Department of Agriculture officials, usually at odds in public, make use of frequent private contacts to avoid getting into an uncontrolled spiral of grievances, retaliation and counter-retaliation. The US Secretary of State, together with three other members of the American cabinet, has an annual meeting with the Commission in December. But in my time no individual did more to ensure that the US and the Community at least understood each other than my American colleague, the US Ambassador to the Community, George Vest. (Incidentally, even if Permanent Representatives are not real ambassadors, the ambassadors to the Community of countries like the United States certainly are).

By comparison, the Community's relations with the other super-power are short on content. There is a general consensus that policy towards Russia must be a combination of unity and firmness on the one hand and reasonable efforts to promote détente on the other. Depending on the circumstances, there are sometimes nuances between member governments as to the right balance, with Greece at the pro-Russian end of the spectrum.

Until comparatively recently, the Soviet Union tried to pretend that the Community did not exist. This did not prevent them entering into discussions about fish after the extension to 200-mile limits in 1976, though nothing came of them when the Russians discovered that the Community would only entertain a reciprocal agreement, not a one-sided one. It is worth remembering that, because the Community was united, the huge Soviet fishing fleet left its new extended waters (where they had been fishing increasingly in recent years) without any fuss. I remember that, at the time, some faint-hearted people in the Foreign Ministries of the Ten foresaw real trouble over this. But the Russians wisely decided that a 'mackerel war' with the Community was not in their interests and faded away at the first Community demand.

The Russians used to try to persuade their East European clients not to enter into direct relations with the Community. When this policy started to crumble, they set out on a new tack and tried to promote an EEC/CMEA agreement despite the fact that the two organisations are very different in their scope. The Community for its part has been ready to make some marginal concessions to those Eastern European countries ready to enter the bilateral agreements. This has produced an EEC/Romanian agreement and some inconclusive discussions with Hungary. As for an EEC/CMEA agreement, the Community is ready to enter into cautious exploratory discussions, but will want to be sure that the Russians do not succeed in using the idea to prevent direct Community relations with the East Europeans. It seems probable that, as a result, Community relations with the Soviet Union and Eastern Europe will soon become 'normalized'!

The countries to whom the Community are closest are the other West European countries of EFTA – Norway, Sweden, Finaland, Iceland, Switzerland, and Austria, with whom the Community has free trade arrangements. The EFTA countries follow what the community does in many ways. But, paradoxically, the Council does not have a lot of EFTA questions on its agenda. The periodical EEC/EFTA meetings lack content, though the Commission does quite a lot of detailed business with them, and work is going on to put more content into the relationship. In a sense, no EFTA news is good news. It means there are no quarrels. But the EFTA countries need to feel engaged with the Community.

With the African, Caribbean and Pacific (ACP) countries of the Lomé Convention, on the other hand, the Community has a close but often acrimonious relationship. The aid and trade advantages the ACP countries secure from it are, as they readily admit, important. But they import into it some of the North/South negotiating techniques of UNCTAD or the UN itself and are always asking for a little more. It is perhaps a subconscious justification for being in some ways part of the Brussels family, which does not always fit easily with the block-to-block approach, particularly of African countries, in North/South negotiations.

Another category of countries who get aid and trade concessions from the Community – but through bilateral agreements, not a group-to-group relationship – are the Mediterranean countries (except for Libya and Albania). They are less favourably treated than the Lomé countries and their agricultural products compete with those of Italy, Greece and now Spain and Portugal. As a result, most of them are constantly forced to struggle, with support from the Community's Northern members, to avoid having their concessions eroded. Cyprus, Malta, Israel, Turkey, Tunisia, Morocco, Yugoslavia, all have grievances and tend to regard the Community as a difficult partner, but they all get substantial benefits from their relationship with it.

In addition to the Lomé and Mediterranean countries, a variety of other countries such as Bangladesh, North Yemen, and Latin American countries, receive Community aid out of the 'aid to non-associates' programme. Considerable quantities of food aid are also provided each year, the bulk going to Africa, though the Commission's doctrine is rightly that developing countries should be helped to grow their own food and not become dependent on food aid imports. Finally, the Community budget keeps funds available for emergency aid to disaster-struck countries, of which each year there always, alas, seem to be some.

With ASEAN (Malaysia, Singapore, Thailand, Indonesia, the Philippines) the Community has a more equal and more harmonious group-to-group relationship. Ministers from the two groups meet each year and discuss both economic and political questions, on both of which they have much in common. Relations with the Arab world, apart from the Maghreb, have not been close. In the 1970s there was a 'Euro/Arab dialogue' and endless meetings were held with little result. For all I know, they still go on. More recently, there has been a slow approach march towards group-to-group relations with the Gulf Cooperation Council. But the road is stony because what Saudi Arabia and the Gulf countries want is free access for the products from their new petro-chemical plants and this the Community is reluctant to accept.

Up to now, relations with Latin America have been a little thin. There is a Latin-American group of ambassadors in Brussels (GRULA) and there have been occasional meetings between it and COREPER. The Community has bilateral agreements with several Latin American countries and group-to-group relations with the Andean Pact and the Central American countries. But there has not been a great deal to show for it. Perhaps the arrival of Spain and Portugal will help to put more content into these various arrangements.

Much time and effort has been devoted to Japan in the last decade, most of it aimed at getting the Japanese to do something about their trade surplus. The Japanese, being extremely hard-headed, are slightly readier to accommodate a common European line than to pay attention to the efforts of individual European governments. But they are, rightly from their point of view, much more worried about the United States, on whom they depend for their security against the USSR and who are more likely to take really damaging action against Japanese exports than the Community. As a result, when they take the sort of minimal action to increase their imports which they judge necessary to stave off combined action against them, the Japanese tend slightly to favour the US, but to stay well short of taking effective measures to reduce their surplus. In my view, the Japanese establishment is being short-sighted in not putting more effort into increasing imports of manufactures, towards which Prime Minister Nakasone has himself pointed the way. In the circumstances, the Community should have a serious try at getting the US Government to take combined action to secure the necessary action.

Finally on this brief and far from comprehensive tour of the Community's foreign policies, we come to South Africa. The Community, like the other industrialised countries, deplores apartheid and wants to contribute to pressure on the South Africans to abolish it. There is an agreed code of conduct for European firms operating in South Africa and in September 1985 the Twelve decided on some modest anti-South African measures. There are nuances of opinion about how far this should go, with Germany and Britain reluctant to push things to the point of economic sanctions which would hurt South African blacks even more than whites and be economically damaging to the bordering African countries. It would also, incidentally, damage the economies of those countries who applied sanctions, substantially in the case of the UK! This issue seems likely to take up a great deal of the Community's time during the 1986 British Presidency and thereafter.

As the reader will deduce from this short round-up – a *tour d'horizon* in classical diplomatic parlance – the Community's priorities, policies and attitudes, are (not surprisingly) rather like those of the United Kingdom. All member states contribute to forming the Community consensus and the UK at least as much as any other. With a little more effort by all concerned, the Community could come a great deal closer to having a common foreign policy across most of the board within the next few years.

But the acute reader will have noted that there were two important dogs which did not bark in this chapter – the international monetary system and defence. In my view, for very different reasons, the Community Governments should be taking more common action in both fields. In the international monetary field I believe that (especially if Britain had joined the ERM of the EMS in 1979) it would have been possible for a Community initiative, modelled in part on the EMS itself, to have led to earlier common action to reverse the absurdly exaggerated dollar rise of 1983/4/early 85 and perhaps to co-operation between Europe, the United States and Japan to manage international exchange rates so as to prevent overshooting in future.

In the defence field, the link with government procurement in general and industrial policy in the Community points strongly to the need for a defence component in the European enterprise. But neither of these subjects can be treated within the scope of this book. I wrote a paper on the case for a European Defence Community to give strength to the European pillar of the Atlantic Alliance when I was at Harvard in 1971. Even then it was not a subject for treatment in a chapter or two and, though I remain unrepentant in my views, I recognize that the complications are in some ways even greater now.

12

Constitutional Issues

THOUSANDS OF PAGES in the newspapers of every member country have been
devoted to Community constitutional issues in the last year or two. But more
heat than light has been generated. Even though a large measure of agreement
was reached at the European Council in Luxembourg in December 1985, it is
worth looking behind all the words to see what the real issues have been.

One main area of confusion has been what is meant by 'progress' in the
Community. Three different strands emerge. When they speak of progress,
some people are thinking of the achievements of greater unity in the world.
The last chapter brought out the considerable degree of unity already achieved
and the possibilities for improvement. There is no theoretical dispute among
the governments about the need for greater unity, which explains the relative
ease with which a draft very close to the original British proposal of May 1985
for a formal political co-operation agreement and a small secretariat in Brussels
was agreed in Luxembourg.

The second strand is only slightly more controversial among the governments, though it worries anti-marketeers in Denmark and Britain. It is the
question whether the Community should be allowed or encouraged to deal
with new subjects and therefore to pass laws in new areas, that is to say, in the
jargon, to extend 'Community competence'. During the life of the Community
there have been many extensions of Community competence under Article
235; the question under consideration in the Intergovernmental Conference
was whether some of these should now be incorporated in new Articles in the
Treaty.

Especially since the European Court laid down in the 1970s that where the
Community has adopted internal rules, it should negotiate internationally as
the Community, there have been pockets of bureaucratic resistance towards
extensions of competence. European officials who are used to negotiating on
their own government's behalf in a large number of international technical
bodies, whether, for example, dealing with shipping or sulphuric emissions

from power stations, do not always relish the thought of Community competence being extended to their field, even if they usually stand a better chance of getting their way in the end as part of a Community team. But no government among the Ten, even the Danes, has been automatically and in principle opposed to extensions of Community competence. Most have been pragmatic about it. If the thing in question needed to be done in the Community, it was done and the consequences for competence were accepted – and little discussed. There was in the end very little controversy about including references to the Regional Fund, the Environment, Research and Technology and even Monetary Capacity in the revised Treaty.

The third strand is much more philosophical and ideological and, had it surfaced as a real split on substance, would have been dangerously controversial. It is the question whether progress in the Community must entail a shift in the balance of its Constitution in the sense of giving more power to the central institutions – the Parliament, the Commission or the Court – at the expense of the Council, that is to say the member governments.

THE PARLIAMENT

This issue underlay many of the discussions about the powers of the European Parliament. Should extensions of Community competence continue to take place only with the consent of all the member governments? If the answer they gave was 'Yes', the governments needed to be careful about giving new powers to the Parliament. To give the European Parliament the last word on legislation, that is to say, to allow the European Parliament to overrule national governments and therefore national parliaments would have been to cross an important threshold in the direction of a federal system as well as risking the passage of some legislation which would not fit in with national laws. MEPs could not be expected to be as careful as national ministers and officials about getting the wording exactly right from the latter point of view.

There are differences of approach among member governments towards the European Parliament. It is, for example, well regarded in Italy and Belgium, but unpopular in Britain (and even more unpopular in Denmark), though the present British Government has worked hard to improve co-operation between the Council and the Parliament. Despite these nuances and despite many Italian, Belgian or even German speeches about the desirability of giving more powers to the Parliament, the fascinating outcome of deep thought by all member governments about what amendments to propose to the Treaties was that the Federalist dog did not bark. Not a single government put forward a proposal to give the Parliament the final say over legislation in any field. The furthest the Italian proposal went – and that was further than anyone else – was to give the Parliament the right to approve or disapprove draft legislation after it had been approved in the Council, that is to say, the Parliament would have been able to kill legislation the Council liked, but not to pass legislation it disliked. It is doubtful if that would have satisfied the Parliament or improved the functioning of the Community. So the Italian proposal gathered no support. The Italians did not, however, dispute the consensus view that the Council must retain the last word on the drafting of legislation which is to be passed. Governments and national parliaments are not ready to allow the European Parliament to pass laws which are directly applicable in their countries without their own consent.

As far as the Parliament was concerned, two other issues arose. Should the Council try to associate it more closely with the process of drafting legislation and, if so, how far would extra delays be acceptable in order to do so? Was it necessary somehow to increase the power of the Parliament in order to deal with a 'democratic deficit'?

To the first question, most governments answered Yes in principle and then divided several ways about what to do. The solution adopted at the European Council in Luxembourg was to introduce a new stage into the process of legislation. Up to now (and until the Treaty is amended), the Parliament has had to give an opinion and, if the Council seemed unlikely to go along with it, could ask for a 'conciliation' meeting. Such meetings have never been a success because the Council has completed its own negotiation before they were held in order to have a 'common position' to discuss with the Parliament – and then naturally has been unable to change anything important in response to the wishes of the Parliament because that would have undone the hard-won compromises which went to make up the common position.

In future, under the Presidency proposal provisionally approved in Luxembourg, after the Council has adopted its common position (on the new issues to be subject to majority voting – see below), the Parliament will have the right to propose precise amendments and, if these are approved by the Commission, the Council can only reject or change them unanimously, though it still needs to be able to muster a qualified majority to approve them. To put it crudely the Council will allow the Parliament to have their say twice, in slightly different ways, but will be under no legal obligation to pay any attention. That is not to say that no attention will be paid. If the Parliament makes good proposals for amendment, which seem sensible to governments and gain support in the media, they will no doubt get approved by both Commission and Council.

Since there are time limits of three months on each of the last two stages, the extra delays should not be excessive, unlike those under the earlier, much more complicated German proposal for a mixed Council/Parliament Committee which still would have left the Council with the last word. But it is doubtful whether the Luxembourg solution will do much to reduce the Parliament's sense of frustration. What its members have been arguing for is a power of 'co-decision' such as exists on the Community budget. For member governments that was not an encouraging precedent.

The Parliament will, in addition, be added to the list of those who have to approve new members of the Community or new Association Agreements under Articles 237 and 238. This will not be regarded as more than a crumb from the Council's table. Neither new members nor new Associates are coming forward in the life of this Parliament. And, to change the metaphor, no one gets much pleasure from being added as a fifth wheel to the coach.

To say that the European Parliament will be dissatisfied is not necessarily to accept that there will be a 'democratic deficit'. It is natural that the European Parliament should seek new powers and have great difficulty in securing them. That is clearly its destiny! It is not like a national parliament in that, among other things, it does not have to approve the raising of revenue – which is the power that most national parliaments have used in the past as a lever to extract yet more power from the Crown. This possibility was debated in 1984 in the context of the amendment of the own resources decision. But the unanimous consensus was that the power to increase own resources must remain with the national governments and parliaments. The governments have not therefore given the European Parliament – and will not lightly give it – any such lever, for they know that it too would use it to extract still more power. So the Parliament may have to struggle on at least for a generation or two, without securing major new powers. But this does not mean either that there is a democratic deficit or that it has no role.

The acts of the Council are decided by democratically elected ministers in accordance with the Community's Constitution, basically the Treaty of Rome. Ministers are subject to control by their own parliaments. It is a matter of political taste and judgement whether to prefer that form of democratic control to control by the European Parliament. For the moment not one member government prefers the latter, and it is they, and their national parliaments, who have the power to give or not to give more powers to the European Parliament under the Treaty. Though no one can know what would happen if the issue were put to a European referendum, we have in my opinion to assume for the time being that the view of the governments represents the democratic will of the people of Europe.

As for a role, the Parliament has certainly increased its influence dramatically since it was first directly elected in 1979. The Commission probably pays more attention to its views than to those of the Council. In the Council itself it now carries a certain weight. It has cleverly, if somewhat unscrupulously, exploited its budgetary powers in increased Community expenditure. It will be able, if it uses the new procedure agreed in Luxembourg equally cleverly, to increase significantly its influence over draft legislation.

To go to the Parliament and see the powerful groups of lobbyists constantly at work there brings home how much more it is perceived as being able to do now than a mere seven years ago. Admittedly these professionals who get paid for their services may have exaggerated not only their own powers of persuasion, but the actual powers of the Parliament itself when they presented their programme of action to their clients. Most trade associations and industrial companies think that the Parliament's role is greater than it is. The Luxembourg solution may mean that their fees to lobbyists are marginally better spent!

Personally, I regret that the British proposal for an improved conciliation procedure which was made before the Milan European Council was not adopted at Luxembourg. This was in essence that the key 'conciliation' meeting between the Council and the Parliament should take place before, not after, the Council has carried out the last stage of its own negotiation and adopted a common position. To do this would be to allow the Parliament to argue its case with ministers at a stage when they could still usefully take its views into account in their final decision. I believe that this proposal would, if adopted and properly followed up by the Parliament, have given it just as great, if not a greater, role in the legislative process as the Luxembourg solution and with less delays in decision-taking. After all, the aim was to make the Community work better, not worse.

But it would not, of course, have increased its powers, only its influence. Nor will the Luxembourg solution. Many Parliamentarians and their Federalist supporters will regard this as sufficient reason to condemn the European Council for making only trivial changes to the Treaty. It seems unlikely that they can generate much wider support, without which the governments will certainly now rest on what they have decided.

MAJORITY VOTING

Majority voting is a more complicated matter, partly because of the controversy over the 'Luxembourg Compromise' of February 1966 (briefly described in Chapter Two). The constitutional aspect is however simple, whether the consent of all the governments and therefore the national parliaments should remain necessary for the passage of laws. If a law could be passed by majority vote, despite the strongly expressed opposition of a member government, it would be an important step in a Federal direction. But there are quite a lot of other issues involved in the debate about majority voting.

It is the constitutional issue which has always underlain the controversy over the Luxembourg Compromise. General de Gaulle was trying to take back a small piece of sovereignty, ceded to the Community when the French National Assembly ratified the Treaty of Rome before he returned to power in 1958. It was not a large piece of sovereignty because the majority voting provisions of the Treaty were carefully designed not to go far in a Federal direction. Unanimity was provided for in most fields where the sovereignty issue arose in an acute form. But General de Gaulle insisted all the same.

The result was formally an agreement to differ. France insisted that discussion should continue, wherever 'very important national interests' were involved, until unanimous agreement was reached. The other Five did not formally accept this, but were careful during the remaining three years of the General's reign not to vote him down. Many people in the other governments in fact took the reasonable view that it would be contrary to the interests of the Community as a whole to ride roughshod over the very important interests of any member state, let alone one as weighty and unpredictable as General de Gaulle's France. But they did not want to give in to him and change the Constitution.

While France was its only supporter, the so-called veto under the Luxembourg Compromise was fragile. The others could, if irritated enough by its abuse on minor issues, have voted France down at any time. But the position changed with the first enlargement. Mr Heath and his government espoused the Gaullist position and the right of veto was overstated in the British debate about entry. The Danish Government were strong, and the Irish Government moderate, supporters of the same position. Greece later joined the British and the Danes. The result was therefore that in practice the veto power became more secure. In the Community of Nine (and Ten) France and Britain together had a blocking minority and could, by supporting each other if one invoked the Compromise, make it effective against its opponents, even without Ireland, Denmark or Greece.

Though more secure, it was not completely safe as Britain found over agricultural prices in 1982, the only occasion when a country invoking the

Compromise has been voted down (see page 100). On that occasion, France and Ireland deserted the camp and made a qualifying majority against Britain possible, since Britain, Greece and Denmark on their own were just short of sufficient votes to block.

During the discussion of the Genscher/Colombo solemn declaration before Stuttgart in 1983 and again before the Milan European Council in June 1985, there was some talk about the possibility of all member states converging on a common position about the Luxembourg Compromise outside the Treaty, under which the right to postpone a vote would have been generally recognised but would have had to be formally justified by the member government concerned in the General Affairs Council or even the European Council. But the Belgians and Italians found even this politically difficult and when the Intergovernmental Conference met to revise the Treaty, the idea faded away. On all sides it was recognised that it would prove impossible to convert the Luxembourg Compromise, or Agreement to Differ, into generally agreed Treaty language.

And so the issue was barely discussed in the Intergovernmental Conference. The situation rests where it has always rested, except that the German Government's position has become equivocal since their repeated invocation of the Compromise in the discussions about cereal prices in the 1985 price-fixing. Will they now support others who invoke it? If not, can they reasonably hope that a blocking minority will support them if they invoke it again? It would certainly seem to be morally and politically difficult for Germany to profit from others' support one year and to vote them down the next.

The accession of Spain and Portugal will also affect the position to some extent, though possibly not very much. The allocation of votes is now as follows:

France	10
Germany	10
Italy	10
UK	10
Spain	8
Netherlands	5
Belgium	5
Denmark	3
Greece	5
Ireland	3

| Portugal | 5 |
| Luxembourg | 2 |

The qualified majority is 54 out of 76 and the blocking minority 23. To get a blocking minority, there have therefore now to be two big countries plus one other (except Luxembourg). On the other hand, it may be that Spain at any rate and perhaps Portugal as well will join the Luxembourg Compromise camp. If so, that camp will emerge strengthened. Even if not, the balance will not be greatly changed, given the position of Germany and the fact that France, Britain and any two others (Denmark, Greece or Ireland) will make a blocking minority.

On the whole, it seems probable that the ability to delay a vote indefinitely will continue with about the same force as before, but that the moral pressure against invoking the Compromise lightly will grow. Its continued existence is a major factor in making it possible for some governments, such as those of Britain, France or Denmark, to agree to the extension of majority voting to new fields because it gives them an answer to anti-Federalist objections. But they do not expect to use it at all often. Indeed, it has seldom been in the foreground when decisions about whether to vote or not to vote have been taken.

The truth is that in the everyday life of the Community majority voting is much less important than it is believed to be outside. There is only a difference of degree in the behaviour of delegations in the Council where unanimity or qualified majority is required. The way the Council works is that a delegation which finds itself in a minority, or still more so if isolated, is expected to compromise as soon as possible. A great deal of pressure is brought to bear and even the Danes, with their Folketing Committee breathing down the government's neck, usually find some way of settling within a month or two.

Ministers much prefer in any case not to vote each other down, unless (which is not unknown) the isolated minister indicates privately to the President that it would be easier for him at home to be voted down than to change his position. So whether the issue is a voting matter or not, quite a lot of effort will be put into securing a compromise if one or two delegations think that the majority position would be damaging to important interests in their country or countries. Until recently, and in some Councils even now, voting has hardly ever taken place, and certainly not if one minister indicates that that would place him in a difficult position. Agriculture ministers, for example, prefer to make up a price-fixing package acceptable to all each year than to have votes.

161

The case of the German use of the Compromise in the Agriculture Council over cereal prices in the 1985 price-fixing is instructive. Most of the other ministers thought that the German minister had gone too far in committing himself so unreservedly to vetoing the smallest decline in Deutschmark prices. So, with great reluctance, they pushed him in the end into invoking the Compromise; and, when he repeatedly did so, they supported the Commission in its decision, by the exercise of its own management powers, to put into effect arrangements equivalent to the last proposal the Germans had vetoed, even though the Germans had prevented the Council from adopting it formally. The Community is a strange animal. Rough justice is usually done. It so happened that in this particular case the Commission was able legally to take equivalent action. That would not, of course, have been the case if primary legislation had been involved.

The position about majority voting has changed a little in the last year or two. The pressure for speeding up decision-making has led people to say that majority voting should be used more often and should gradually become the normal practice as it has always been, even in 1966, in the Budget Council. This has led to a few more votes being taken in the General Affairs Council – against France, for example, in order to allow the Community to adopt a common position on export credits for negotiation with other industrialized countries in the OECD. The knowledge that a problem may be settled by majority vote may sometimes bring about an earlier compromise. Some German officials say, for example, that individual ministries in Bonn are ready for their delegation to be much less inflexible in negotiation if they are told that they may otherwise be voted down.

I do not therefore underestimate the importance of adding new subjects to the list of those to which majority voting applies. Provided on the one hand that the pressure is kept up to make majority voting, where provided for in the Treaty, the normal thing rather than the exception and, on the other, that the majority do not ride roughshod over the very important national interests of the minority, it should do good to enlarge the scope for majority decisions. The second proviso is as important as the first. It cannot be in the interests of the Community, even if it does speed up decision-taking to some extent, to turn this or that member government and its national parliament into a recalcitrant member by overriding its very important national interests.

The discussions in the Intergovernmental Conference have shown how sensitive governments are to the politics of voting. The British and the Irish cannot, for example, contemplate suggesting to their parliaments that they should accept the theoretical possibility of being voted down on the movement of plants or animals, for fear of the Colorado beetle or rabies. The Germans are equally determined about taxation, the Danes about maintaining their environmental standards; and so on. All these are countries that have invoked the Luxembourg Compromise and could in theory reply on that to stop undesirable legislation, but still they cannot agree to majority voting in these fields. It is therefore of considerable significance, at least in political terms, that the consensus in the European Council should now be in favour of majority voting for most issues affecting the creation of the single market. When the amendments have been ratified, majority voting will apply to Articles 28; 57(2), second sentence; 59, second paragraph; 70(1) and 84; as well as to the main body of subjects dealt with under Article 100, except for fiscal provisions, free movement of persons and the rights and interests of employed persons. The exceptions are relatively few in number.

But let no one think that the Community world will be radically changed. The possibility of majority voting will sometimes produce earlier compromises. Occasionally a member government which does not have very important interests at stake will be outvoted. But it will make much more difference to the speed of decision-making if the Commission and the Presidency of the day have the energy and will-power, and the co-operation of main governments concerned with each issue, to prepare behind the scenes each month ways in which the intractable problems can be solved. What will be decisive is whether the general consensus in the Community in favour of pushing on quickly to the single great market continues to strengthen. If it does, the barriers will come down whether the Council votes or not.

THE FUTURE OF THE CONSTITUTIONAL DEBATE

In Luxembourg, the Heads of Government have thus reached a consensus on two of the most controversial issues, the role of the Parliament and majority voting. They have also brought the Treaty up to date by agreeing to include in it references to some of the things which have over the years been added to the community agenda without having a Treaty basis, such as the environment, technology, the Regional Fund and the EMS. They have agreed to formalise their obligations in political co-operation. All this, taken together, marks a modest but significant step forward towards greater integration.

Provided that the national parliaments all ratify the Treaty amendments worked out to give effect to this agreement, the constitutional debate should now be muted, if not stilled, for a few years. For the process for seriously considering Treaty changes, as well as the final agreement reached, have brought governments closer together. When they took a serious look at the Treaty in order to decide whether to propose amendments in the Inter-governmental Conference, they all found, including those who had argued most strongly for the Conference, that they did not in fact want to put forward proposals for really radical changes. The Treaty had stood the test of time. This was a useful and unforeseen side-effect of the decision to hold the Conference, a decision which Britain opposed because we did not foresee the outcome.

Of coure, in a few years' time, that fact may be forgotten by a new generation of ministers and officials who may come to think once more that the solution to the Community's problems should be found in tinkering with its Constitution. Meanwhile it will be nice to have a respite. For the past decade, the Community has suffered from a series of self-examinations.

In 1974, Mr Tindemans (then Prime Minister of Belgium) was asked on a French initiative to produce a report on European Union. This he did and the document was on the whole a good one, if a little too Federalist in flavour for the French taste – which was presumably the reason why they made sure that there was no follow-up. Then there was the report of the Three Wise Men (alas, memory fails me about who they were, or indeed who asked them to report) whose excellent report on improving the Community was carefully studied in the Council in 1980 and some useful conclusions adopted by the European Council itself (more honoured since in the breach than the observance). Then the 30th May Mandate (see Chapter Seven) led to a wearing six-month review of all the Community's policies (in addition to the budget problem), but the practical results were meagre. Then there was the Genscher/Colombo initiative on European Union which led after a year's negotiation to the Solemn Declaration of June 1983 which sank immediately without a trace. And, finally, there was the Committee under Professor Dooge (ex-Irish Foreign Minister) which met as a result of another French initiative, this time by President Mitterrand at Fontainebleau, in the autumn of 1984 and early 1985 and produced a rather superficial report – in parallel with another Committee on a People's Europe, also set up at Fontainebleau, which produced a few small but useful proposals for action to improve the Community's impact on the common man. None of these exercises produced results commensurate with the time and energy devoted to them. Indeed it has not always been possible to stifle the suspicion that some people, whether consciously or not, found such broad discussions a satisfactory alternative to getting down to taking the really difficult specific decisions, for example on the internal market or the reform of the CAP. Perhaps it is not too much to hope that the time and energy saved by not discussing the future of the Community as a whole will go to improve its future piecemeal.

Alongside these discussions, and sometimes as part of them, a coded debate has been taking place about ends, not means. No one is arguing that the ultimate destination of the journey the member states are making together should now be defined. Most ministers and officials have long since tacitly agreed that it would be useless and divisive to try to spell out a Constitutional aim. A Federation? A directly-elected President of a European executive? A Confederation (whatever that may be)? It is best to leave these questions aside.

But, for political reasons, it is not easy for ministers everywhere to avoid taking a position. Mrs Thatcher, if questioned in the House of Commons (and sometimes even if not) will say that she cannot conceive of there ever being a United States of Europe, by which presumably she means of Europe becoming something like the United States of America. Mr Tindemans of Belgium or Signor Andreotti of Italy might easily find it politically necessary to assert the contrary, though I am not sure if they have.

For some years, this clash of views was defused, and indeed diffused, by setting the aim of 'European Union' as a common goal. This was done at the October 1972 Paris Summit of the Nine, just before the first enlargement, which declared in its communiqué that the member states were going to transform the whole complex of their relations into a European Union (the phrase sounded better in French). This magical name has been reiterated in subsequent solemn documents and declarations by Heads of Government on innumerable occasions, most solemnly and categorically in the solemn Declaration of 1983. 'European Union' has had the supreme advantage of ambiguity. Those in front crying 'forward' could speak as though it meant a Federation. Those behind crying 'back' could point out that seven members of the Community had been members of Western European Union for thirty years and of the European Postal Union for longer still. Nothing Federal about a Union!

In 1985 this helpful ambiguity was put at risk. France and Germany tabled a draft Political Co-operation Treaty before the Milan European Council which said explicitly that European Union, consisting of the Community and political co-operation, would exist on the day the draft was signed. This might have been acceptable to the British, who did not wish to exaggerate the scope of the oft-repeated commitment to European Union. To say that it already exists would put an end to the debate about what might need to be done to attain it. But it was politically much less attractive to those such as Italy and the Benelux who prefer to argue that much still needs to be done before this distant good can be clearly seen, let alone reached. The Luxembourg Presidency's draft 'Single Act' approved by Foreign Ministers in January 1986 came down on the side of the distant good – the Community and political co-operation 'shall have as their objective to contribute together to making concrete progress towards European unity'. (Incidentally, the word used in the other languages was 'union' not 'unity'. The explanation offered is that the latter word was used in English because it was explicitly recognised that 'union' can be taken in English to mean a fixed constitutional state whereas, like 'unity' in English, in the other languages it can and often does mean a process.)

So the debate about what needs to be done to establish European Union or unity will be able to continue. Ideological positions will be taken up, attacked and defended. This is a phenomenon which is not uncommon when new political systems are invented. The Russian Communists have their 'dictatorship of the proleteriat' and 'the withering away of the state'. Europeans have European Union.

Even if most old Community hands would agree that we should leave the question of the destination of the journey we are making together unanswered, there is another to which they seek a reassuring answer. Is the Community process now irreversible? Many feel that if they assert that is, that will make it so. Though that is a doubtful proposition, I believe that they are safe to claim irreversibility.

Sometimes during the last ten years the Europessimists seemed for a time to be in the ascendant. They asserted, wrongly at every period, that the Community was blocked – there was always progress going on somewhere. They were afraid that resurgent nationalism might undermine the 'construction of Europe'. But when the Heads of Government felt this danger, when they looked down into the abyss which would swallow them if they failed to solve their problems, they hurried quickly back to the European Council table and hammered out an agreement. They knew in their very political hearts that they were condemned to agree.

As my colleagues in London and Brussels will bear witness, I never fell victim to Europessimism, which seemed indeed to me to be contrary to all the evidence. For I believe that the Community has long since assumed a life of its own. If it could in its early years resist General de Gaulle's desire to replace it with intergovernmental co-operation between sovereign states, twenty years and immense progress later it can easily cope with its much less formidable opponents of the present day.

Of course, in one sense it is still dependent on the will of the members, the member states, to maintain it. It is less secure than the Federal institutions in the United States. It is still just conceivable that Denmark or Greece or even the UK could drop out. But, first, I do not believe that the Danish, Greek or British people, when faced with the choice, would ever choose the exit. The Danish referendum on the draft Treaty amendments of 27 February, 1986, confirms me in this view, as well as demonstrating how difficult it is for any member state to swim against the Community tide. Second, I am certain that if one or more members did, for their own idiosyncratic reasons, leave, the others would close ranks and work still harder to heal the wound and keep the processes of integration going.

Moreover, there is another sense in which the Community has achieved an independent existence. Its institutions have a certain strength and have now been part of the constitution of the original member states for a generation. The now huge body of the Community law could not easily or quickly be replaced. But, still more important, a powerful constituency backs the Community in every member state. I do not believe that anyone wishing to destroy the Community could acquire sufficient power even to stem the tide of its progress. It is in this sense that I say that it has a life of its own.

But while I am confident that the Community will continue to move forward, I do not even have a personal view about its constitutional destination. The world will continue to get smaller. In order to create a new international monetary system, the main industrialised countries need to start sharing sovereignty in very much the way that this happens in the Community because it has to be done if the problems are to be solved. For high technology products Europe is already only an important part of a quasi-global market, which could become a genuine single great market, at least of the industrialised countries. Increasingly the world's financial markets are becoming a single global market. Who can know whether our children or great-grandchildren will be continuing the process of European integration by electing a President of Europe by universal suffrage, joining as a Community with the United States and Japan in creating a triangular directorate of the countries of industrialised world – or going further or less far? In the real world, there are no absolute or ultimate objectives – only change, for better or for worse. Who can seriously argue that the progress towards European unity so far made has not helped to banish war between Western European countries, promote our prosperity and allow us to solve together many problems which are crying out for solutions, while doing nothing to destroy the desirable aspects of our diversity?

The whole world needs better international co-operation if its problems are to be resolved and disasters avoided. The Community is setting a good example. To go on doing so it does not need to be able to say where it will be in 2000, or 2058 on its hundredth anniversary. It is enough for it to keep moving.

Conclusion

When I was a child before the Second World War and the British Empire was still largely intact, it was reasonable, but perhaps no longer right, to believe the history books which told us that Britain was a Great Power. After the war, as the two superpowers emerged dominant in their own spheres of influence, and powerful everywhere, and as Britain started to shed its empire, it was careless of our leaders not to notice straight away that our role had to change. It is sad that when Jean Monnet and his friends invented the European *engrenage* we should have thought that it was not for us. We ought to have joined with them to give a lead. Instead we scarcely noticed how new and important the European idea was.

So we missed the first bus, the Coal and Steel Community, and the second bus, the EEC itself. Mr Macmillan tried to clamber on in 1961 but General de Gaulle, after a bit of a tussle, was able to push him off. Mr Wilson and Mr George Brown never even got their foot on the step in 1966/67. When we did join in 1973, we did so pretending that General de Gaulle's version of Europe, co-operation between wholly sovereign states, had won the day, whereas in truth it had failed to break the Community mechanism and the process of integration was picking up speed again. Moreover, we joined with handicaps like New Zealand butter, fish and the budget inequity which were to absorb so much of our energy and our negotiating skills in our first twelve years of membership. At last these issues no longer place us apart and we are on equal terms with the other members. What should we conclude?

Europe is now more than a continent. But European integration is, in its everyday life, primarily about solving detailed, complicated and usually technical problems by consensus in a political framework which makes it extremely difficult for governments to do other than agree in the end. That is what makes it so interesting and so unique. So we should set about solving problems. Alas, there is no shortage of them.

To name only a few, the ECOFIN Council must address itself to the

169

maintenance and enlargement of the EMS zone of monetary stability and will do well, in my view, to take the initiative with the United States, Japan and others to create a more stable international monetary system in which the world's currencies are collectively managed to avoid over-shooting.

The ECOFIN Council, and many other Councils, must do what they can to contribute to raising the European economic growth rate above the rate of growth of productivity (without reducing the latter) and thus slowly begin to bring the rate of unemployment down. That is very difficult.

The Agriculture Council must somehow, and soon, find the will to halt the growth of the CAP surpluses and begin gradually to bring them down. That, too, is almost impossibly difficult – and yet it must be done if expenditure on agriculture is not to put an impossible strain on the Community budget and thus risk the destruction of the CAP, reopening old quarrels in the process.

The Environment Council must make a major contribution to ending acid rain, cleaning European rivers and lakes, preventing our seas from being choked with pollution – and do all this without imposing unacceptably large burdens on industry in comparison with the regulatory burden in the United States or Japan.

The Internal Market Council (only invented in 1983) must take the lead, with other Councils, in creating a single market by 1992.

The Industry, Research and General Affairs Councils must tackle the question of how to help European high technology companies to co-operate in order to survive in a global market against the American and Japanese competition, without contributing to the outbreak of economic warfare between the allies on both sides of the Atlantic.

The General Affairs Council must somehow keep the trade quarrels with the United States under control.

Both in the Community itself and in political co-operation the Twelve must apply some of their stock of will-power to avoiding marching off in different directions, as they did over SDI, and to taking more effective common positions in world affairs.

I name only a small number of the problems which are crying out for imaginative solutions in the Council. Every day eight working groups will meet to deal with eight such problems, every month six councils. Britain is doing good work in most of them, but could do more to recognise the significance not only of all these efforts, taken together, but also of the Community itself. For almost no one in Britain recognises that something new and exciting is happening to the old Continent. Its ancient nations are learning, almost certainly have learnt, to leave behind them for ever insistence on the unfettered sovereignty of the nation state. Through the mechanisms of the Community, invented to make the sharing of sovereignty easy, they are co-operating to solve not only Europe's but the world's problems through sharing yet more sovereignty as the solutions to the problems demand. In the process they take more decisions every month than are taken in a year in all the many other international organisations to which they belong put together. The reason that public lack of recognition matters is that the problems are so many and so urgent that the governments need the support of a little public enthusiasm if they are to act fast enough to reverse Europe's decline, save the environment and strengthen the western world.

Alas! I do not believe in miracles. Controversy in and about the Community will continue to rage for as long as the Community is a live and dynamic organisation. Out of the controversy, ministers and officials will grind compromises. In some walks of life it is a sin to compromise. In the Community it is often a sin not to.

Only the Communist and crypto-Communist Left and the extreme Right can even contemplate trying to reverse the Community tide. The Left have to do so because a successful Community will be the strongest barrier to the sort of regimented 'people's democracy', guided by themselves, that they dream in vain of establishing in Western European countries. The extreme Right long to do so because they too dream, but of a long-lost world (if it ever existed) where the sovereignty of every nation was untrammelled by the need to live with others.

Neither vision is realistic. The cogs of the European *engrenage* continue methodically to turn, making the process of European integration more and more irreversible every year. No serious European country can afford to drop out. There is no alternative to slogging on. The British people, who always grumble about their own government, will no doubt continue to grumble about the European Community. But I believe that many of the grumblers have accepted in their inmost thoughts that it is here to stay and must be made to work.

Making Europe work better will never seem glamorous and will often be painful to those whose job it is to keep the wheels turning. I take a lot of satisfaction from having spent so long sweating away in Europe's engine-room. I cannot claim to have changed the course of history. Luckily, perhaps, no individual in modern Europe can hope to do much of that. But I have certainly felt party to history in the making. For the historians will, I believe, say that the Community *engrenage*, invented by that great European, Jean Monnet, was

171

one of the most significant and beneficial contributions of the old Continent to the post-war world.

Index

compiled by Richard M. Wright

173